Cornish is Fun!

an informal course
in living Cornish

Heini Gruffudd
ed. Ray Chubb

catroons by Elwyn Ioan

yLolfa

Front cover: Robat Gruffudd/Elwyn Ioan
Back cover photograph courtesy of the Cornwall Tourist
Board

ISBN: 0 86243 659 1

Printed and published in Wales
by Y Lolfa Cyf., Talybont, Ceredigion SY24 5AP
e-mail ylolfa@ylolfa.com
website www.ylolfa.com
tel. (01970) 832 304
fax 832 782

How to use this book

1   This book will give you a good start in learning to speak Cornish. After you've been through the lessons, and know the vocabulary at the end, you'll be able to say quite a lot of things —enough to hold your own in a conversation. A whole new Cornish world lies before you.

2   Go through the lessons one by one. Master one before going on to the next.· Read them all aloud. Do the exercises, and make up your own sentences, using the words you will already have learnt in previous lessons. If possible, get a Cornish speaker to help. UNDERSTAND each lesson before going on to the next.

3   Use your Cornish whenever you can. Find a friend to learn it with you. In case of difficulty, you can say:
Cows yn-lent —Speak slowly. Dysky a' wrama—I do learn.
Ny gonvedhaf—I don't understand. Arta mar" plêk? —
(Repeat that please?...i.e. What did you say?)
But don't lapse into English, or you'll find yourself speaking more English and less Cornish.

4   Why not buy a Cornish dictionary? ·

5   When you have finished this book, there are others, bigger ones, if you want to study more. For the spoken language there is Kernewek Es ; for a more grammatical approach there is Cornish for Beginners, and, more advanced, Cornish Simplified. A lively and inexpensive companion to CORNISH IS FUN is Lyver Lavarow Kernewek (a phrase book)*

6   If you live in Cornwall, you could get in touch with others interested in Cornish by contacting the Secretary of Agan Tavas .

7   If you enjoy Folk Music, you can often hear songs in Cornish at St Ives Folk Club.
8   Of course, try to join any Cornish class: private, Tech., or W.E.A. Again, Agan Tavas will help.

9   However, if your aim is just to know enough Cornish to have some fun in the language around Cornwall, in cafe, pub, dance, football match, home etc., then this book is good enough on its own. Why not buy one for a friend?

NOTE* If your bookseller has no Cornish stock (in which case he should try to move with the times), a list of available books, discs etc. can be obtained from: Spyrys a Gernow,iva an Chy Gordon, Sunnyvale Rd., Portreath, Redruth TR16 4NE.

Basic Pronunciation

The stress of Cornish words is generally on the last syllable but one. For example: Pysc<u>A</u>jor, fisherman. Where there are exceptions, or possible confusion, the stress will be shown in the vocabulary at the end of this book, using an accent for the stressed vowels.

All consonants are normally pronounced, but tend to be rather lightly sounded at the end of a word.

Vowels have a long and a short sound. In this book, the long value will be shown in the vocabulary by means of an accent.

Here is the Cornish Alphabet:

<u>a</u> – as in "cat". Sometimes as in "ah"
<u>â</u> – as in "Same"...but as said in W. Cornwall rather like a drawn out "i" – ."siiim"
<u>b</u> – normal
<u>c</u> – as "k"
<u>ch</u> – as in "cherry"
<u>d</u> – normal
<u>dh</u> – as "th" in "bathe"
<u>e</u> – as in "get"
<u>ê</u> – as "ai" in "main", but nearer to French é
<u>ey</u> – as "i" in "bike"
<u>eu</u> & <u>ew</u> – as "e-oo"
<u>f</u> – normal, but very slight when not stressed at the end of a word, and as "v" after a stressed vowel.
<u>g</u> – normal
<u>gh</u> – as a breathed "h". Scarcely heared in middle of a word.
<u>h</u> – normal
<u>j</u> – as in "just"
<u>k</u> – normal
<u>l</u> – normal, but with tongue against top teeth.
<u>m</u> – normal, but tends to be <u>bm</u> after short, stressed vowels.

6

n - normal, but tend to be dn after
     short, stressed vowels.
o - as in "hot", but at end of word,
     and in ogh, as "oh!"
ô - as "aw" in some words, as "oo"
     in others. Sorry about that!
ow - a very soft "oo" when unstressed.
     When stressed, is "e-oo".
oy - as "oo-ee"
p - normal, but tends to soften to
     a b at end of word
qu - as in "quiet"
r - lightly rolled. Not so strong
     as in 'Mummerset':
s - as in "hiss"; or as in "his"
     particularly after a stressed
     vowel.
sh - normal
t - normal
th - as in "thin"
u - similar to French "u"
     Nearest English equivalent
     is "ee"
û - as in "oo", or sometimes as
     "ee-oo". (in one or two words,
     as "oo" in Southern pron "cook"
V - normal except when unstressed
     within word when tends to be w
w - normal
wh - breathed, as though "hw"
y - as "i" in "pin"
ŷ - as "ee" in "seen". Sometimes
     as in ey above.
yw - in many words is also a consonant,
     as in "yet".

NOTE: aw is treated as a short â as in "cat", followed by
"w".

INTONATION: Cornish intonation is distinctive, but cannot
be described in print. Discs and tapes available could help
you.

In the first few lessons, the pronunciation is put in brackets.
A small number against a word (e.g. Pur2) indicates the
causing of mutation —see appendix.

NOW BEGIN...........

Some Greetings

pur^2—very (softens some following
  letters; see list at back)
lowr—enough (follows word)
dhe^2—to, at (softens as does pur^2)
kê!—go! (sg)
kê dhe^2 gerdhes! —be off with you!
  (lit.—go to walk!)

y'n chŷ—inside
bal—pest, nuisance
omma—here

SAY & TRANSLATE

Dynargh...........................
Dus y'n chŷ........................
Fat'l ôsta?........................
Da lowr, sôs......................
Dêth da dhys......................

Kê dhe^2 gerdhes!...................
Dus omma..........................
Pur^2 dha........................
Da, murasta.......................
Dew Genes ....

9

An Gewer

Hŷ—she, it
yû—is
uthek—terrible
yeyn—cold
tom—warm

marthus—wonderful
Gast!—general swear word
comolek—cloudy
a² wra—it does; it makes

SAY & TRANSLATE

Myttyn da!........................	Comolek yû hŷ.....................
Yeyn yû hŷ.......................	Marthus brâf yû hŷ................
Glaw a²wra.......................	Nôs da!..........................
Brâf yû hŷ.......................	Tom yû hŷ........................

Y'n Dewottŷ

an coref ŷu...—the beer is...
ha—and
ha'n—and the
an—the
yû hŷ—she/it is
yûa—he/it is
a² wrava—he does

1—onen; (un before noun)
2—deu²
3—trŷ³
4—peswar (pejar)
5—pymp
6—whêgh (hway'h)
7—seyth (sighth)
8—êth—(ayth)

12

SAY & TRANSLATE

Tom yû hŷ...........................
pŷnta.............................
un pŷnta..........................
medhow yûa.......................

pŷnta.............................
An coref yû yeyn..................
An dewottŷ yû yeyn...............
Eva lowr a^2 wra Yowan.............

Y'n Car-tân

10—dêk
20—ugans
30—dêk war'n ugans
40—deugans
50—dêk ha deugans
60—trŷ³ ugans
70—dêk ha trŷ³ ugans
80—peswar ugans
90—dêk ha peswar ugans
100—cans

otomma—here is
otena—there is
mŷ a² wra—I do, I will
y'n—in the
dhe²'n—
bys yn—to, up to, as far as
an—the
an voren a² wra—the girl does

14

3

Mŷ a² wra rŷ dhys deu² buns.
I'LL GIVE YOU TWO POUNDS.

Murasta. Otomma dha² vona: dêk dynar ha peswar ugans.
THANKS. HERE'S YOUR CHANGE: 90p.

4

Mŷ a² wra whetha'n bondow - rôs.
I'LL BLOW UP THE TYRES.

PUMP

RÔS (RAWZ) WHEEL

7

Mŷ a² wra môs bys yn Pen Sans.
I'M GOING TO PENZANCE.

8

Kefnysor* a² wra dôs dhe² 'n car.
A COPPER'S COMING TO THE CAR.

Note: an softens the first letter of some feminine words: for example moren—girl; an voren—the girl

"a" and "some" are not usually expressed
rôs—a wheel, dowr—some water

dôs —come
môs —go
gorra—put

*abusive

SAY & TRANSLATE

Mŷ a² wra trŷ³ galon petrol y'n car
....
Mŷ a² wra rŷ dhys dêk puns war² 'n ugans
....
An² voren a² wra mones bys yn Pol Fenton
....
Dhe² 'n car.............................
Y'n carjŷ.............................
Otomma dowr.............................

15

Y'n Gwestŷ

---

mŷ—I
tŷ—you (sg)
ef—he, it
hŷ—she, it
nŷ—we
whŷ—you (pl&formal)
ŷ—they
a² garsa—would like
a² wra—does, (will) do
yû—is, am, are

dyworth—from
rak—for, in order
pup—each
puponen—each one
ŷ stevel—his room
kemeres—take
cusca—sleep
(Note: what a person is
must be mentioned before
the being...for example:

ôf; ôf vŷ; oma—I am
ôs; ôs jŷ; ôsta—You are
yû; yû ef; yûa—He is
yû; yû hŷ; yûy—She is
on; on nŷ;—We are
ough; ough whŷ—You are
yns; yns ŷ—They are

A-var on nŷ—Early are we)

16

(Note: this set cannot be used for 'being' in a place, only for who or what a person is or is like)

SAY & TRANSLATE

Mŷ a² wra cusca.........................

Mŷ a² wra cusca marthus da...............

Hŷ yû tom stevel.........................

Ef yû helergh y'n gwestŷ.................

Tom yû gwelŷ deublek.....................

Nŷ a² wra dos dyworth Towan Porth Lystry

Y a² wra dos dyworth Lulyn ....

A-var ough whŷ.........................

Y'n Kyttryn

Asking Questions

Eva
Whetha
Gorra   a^2 wrama? —do I?
Whylas   a^2 wrêta? —do you?
Costya   a^2 wrava? —does he?
Kemeres   a^2 wrahŷ? —does she?
Cusca   a^2 wrên nŷ? —do we?
Môs   a^2 wreugh whŷ? —do you?
Dôs   a^2 wrons ŷ? —do they?

Gwraf, Na^2 wraf—I do, I don't
Gwrêth, Na^2 wrêth—You do...
Gwra, Na^2 wra—etc
Gwron, Na^2 wron
Gwrên, Na^2 wrên
Gwreugh, Na^2 wreugh
Gwrons, Na^2 wrons

NOTE by omitting the question mark,
or by adjusting one's tone, the above
set is also used to mean, I do; he does,
etc...as statements. e.g.

18

Dones a wrama—Come I do OR Do I come?
BUT To make a statement, you MUST
mention the action before you say a wrama,
a wrava, etc
    To make a question, put the action
either side—Eva a wrava? A wrava eva?
both mean: "Does he drink?" The first
is better.

11—unnek; 12—deudhek; 13—tredhek;
14—peswardhek; 15—pymthek; 16—
whetek; 17—seytek; 18—ètek; 19—
nawnjek. NOTE:2=deu2(de-oo) but is

SAY & TRANSLATE

An forth ewn yû homma? . . . .
Nag yû . . . Yû . . . .
A wra an kettrŷn dones? . . . .
Na^2 wra . . . . Gwra . . . .
Py cost yû? . . . .
Môs a wrên nŷ? . . . .
Na wrên . . . . Gwrên . . . .
Dôs a wrêta? . . . .
Gwraf . . . . Na^2 wraf . . . .
Pymp dynar ha trŷ ugans . . . .

19

Y'n Gwerthjy

torth—loaf
cafas—tin
Mŷ a garsa—I'd like
pôs—pound (weight)
puns—pound (money)
costrel—bottle

SAY & TRANSLATE

Mŷ a² garsa cafas a² hern..........................
Pôs a² amanyn......................................
Torth a² vara.....................................
Gwertha coref a² wreugh why? ....
Na² wrên; gwertha lêth a² wrên nŷ.................

Y'n Drê‘

p'ur a² wra?...—what time does?
ple⁵ ma?—where is/are?
ymá—is/are (for place where
roy dhym—give me (sg)
nessa—nest/nearest
Gaf dhym   —Excuse me
a⁄—at/for (of prices)

22

SAY & TRANSLATE

An bôstŷ yû ygor dhe² bymp ur...

Ple⁵ 'ma Lŷs an Drê?..

Ple⁵ 'ma'n caughjŷ?*..

Pŷ gost yû cafas tê?..

Gaf dhym! . . . .

Roy dhym tokyn a dheu dhynar ha deugans...........................

*impolite

23

yth esof vŷ—I am
yth esos jŷ—you are
ymá ef—he is
ymá hŷ—she is
yth eson nŷ—we are
yth esough whŷ—you are
ymóns ŷ—they are

This set must·be
used either for being
in a place or with ow[4]
(see table of mutations
in appendix) plus an
action to give an idea
of continuity.

us:–are/is there? OR yes, there is/are
nag us—no, there is/are not
pleth esough whŷ?—Where are you?
dyndyl—earn
hep—without
ple'ma—where is/are?
honna—that (fem)
henna—that (masc)
usy—that is/are

SAY & TRANSLATE

Pleth esos ow^4 quŷtha?.....................
Yth esof ow^4 quŷtha y'n pol-prŷ.............
Yth esof ow^4 tyndyl un puns war^2'n...........
ugans a'n seythen..........................
Ymá peswar cans ow^4 cwŷtha ena.............
Ymá lŷes ena,...............................
Us whêl-stên yn Lanúst?.....................

Y'n Bôsty

1

Kemeres hansel a vynnough whý?
TAKE BREAKFAST WILL YOU?

Na vynnyn, pensogh. Prýs tê yú.
WE WILL NOT, CHUCKLEHEAD, TEA TIME IT IS.

2

Ha mŷ, ny vynnaf kemeres tê; Kemeres cafe y fynnaf vŷ.

AND I DO NOT WISH TO TAKE TEA; TAKE COFFEE I WILL.

5

Mŷ, ny garaf bara'manyn, ha nŷ, ny geryn têsen, hag....

I DO NOT LIKE BREAD AND BUTTER, AND WE DO NOT LIKE CAKE, AND....

6

g, ny garons cowl, ha hŷ, ny gar crâs....

THEY DO NOT LIKE SOUP, AND SHE DOES NOT LIKE TOAST...

Scala SHALLOW BOWL

Collel KNIFE

Forgh FORK

Podyk JUG

WANTING & WILLING

Will I?		Vynnaf vŷ
Do you want to?	a^2 +	vynta jŷ
Does he want to?		vyn êf
I don't want to		vyn hŷ
you don't want to	ny^2 +	vynnyn nŷ	+ action, object etc.
she will not		vynnough whŷ
		vynnons ŷ
Don't I want to?		
Don't you want to?	a ny^2 +	
won't he?		

LIKING

Do I like?		garaf vŷ
Does he like?	a^2 +	geryth jŷ
		gar êf
I don't like)		gar hŷ
You don't like)	ny^2 +	geryn nŷ	+ action object
Don't I like?		gerough whŷ
Doesn't she like?)	a ny^2 +	garons ŷ

26

The above sets can be used to express what you want, what you like, OR what you want/like to do: provided that you mention first the thing you like or want to do; for example Mones dhe'n gwestỹ a⁺vynnyn nŷ—Go to the hotel we will, Tesen a⁺garaf vŷ—Cake I like NOTE—vŷ, jŷ. etc. should be added when asking a question, otherwise they are optional, although very common.
NOTE To express "Yes I will" use Mynnaf, "No I won't" Na⁺vynnaf. Similarly Caraf. Na garaf...

NOTE It is also possible, and EASY to say: mŷ a⁺vyn, êf a⁺vyn, whŷ a⁺vyn, tŷ a⁺gar, ŷ a⁺gar, etc.
But these must not be used in questions or with not.

SAY & TRANSLATE

Mŷ, nŷ⁺vynnaf kemeres tê...........
Mŷ a⁺vyn kemeres cras ha kyfŷth.....
Kemeres cras ha kyfŷth a⁺vynnaf vŷ..
Nŷ a⁺vyn kemeres cowl............
Kemeres cowl a⁺vynnyn nŷ..........
Mŷ a⁺vyn kemeres cafe, bara, amanyn, cowl......................
A⁺nŷ⁺gerough whŷ puber?...........
A⁺nŷ⁺vynnons ŷ kemeres sugra ......

Corf ha Dyllasyow

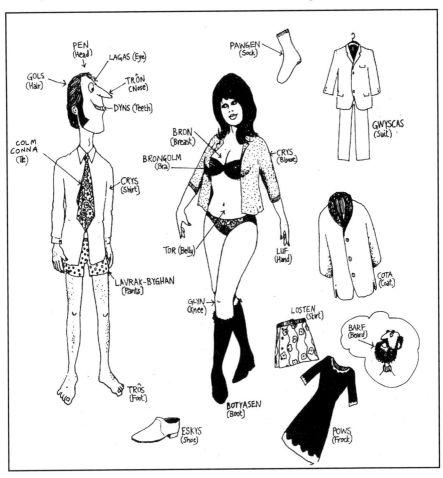

Ym<u>á</u> (there is)
<u>Us?</u> (Is there?)
<u>Nyns us</u>. (there is not)

<u>dhym</u>—to me
<u>dhys</u>—to you
<u>dhodho</u>—to him   I have
<u>dhedhy</u>—to her i.e. you have
<u>dhyn</u>—to us   he has
<u>dheugh</u>—to you
<u>dhedha</u>—to them

NOTE: <u>Us</u>—yes, there is/are. <u>Nyns us</u>
—there isn't. <u>Nag us</u>—No, there isn't.

SAY & TRANSLATE

Us cota dhys?......................

Ymá cryspows dhym.................

Us..............................

Nag us..........................

Nag us; nyns us cota dhym..........

Us losten dhedhy?.................

Us dyllasyow dhedha...............

Us colmow conna genough? ....

Y'n Lytherjŷ

Ymá	genef—I have
Us?	genes—you have
Nyns us	ganso— etc.
	Gensy
	genen
	genough
	gansa

This set is used to denote having
with one, rather than actual possession.

Ymá lyther dhym—I've got a letter
(says recipient)
Ymá lyther dhys—I've got a letter
says the postman)
a^2—of, for
ow mós—going
ná!—no!
maylyer—envelope
hep mar—of course
na vynnaf—no thanks
a'gaf vŷ—can I? may I?
pellgows—to phone
pandr' us...?—what is there?
pandra?—what?
pyü—who?

SAY & TRANSLATE

A² vynnough whŷ cafos stamp?

....

Na² vynnaf..........................

Mŷ a² vyn pellgows..................

Pyû a² vyn pellgows nessa?.........

Us post ow⁴ môs   dhe² whêgh ur?

....

Us, hep mar......................

Pŷ² gost yû maylyer ha stamp?

Pandr' us war² an stamp? ....

Usy'n post ow⁴ mones haneth?........

....

Us post ow³ môs   hedhyû? ....

....

Ples' ma'n pellgows nessa? ....

....

31

Y'n Dôns

a^2?	allaf vŷ	I can or can I?	Da yû genef—Good is with me (I like)
ny^2	ylta jŷ	You can or can you?	Da'vŷa genef—Good would be with me
a ny^2?	ŷl êf	(refer. lesson 10)	(I like)
	ŷl hŷ		Gwell yû genef—Better is with me
	yllyn nŷ		(I prefer)
	yllough whŷ		Gwell'vŷa genef—Better would be with
	yllons ŷ		me (I'd prefer)

3

Dônsya man ny² ylta, mes amma a² ylta brâf.
DANCE AT ALL YOU CANNOT, BUT KISS YOU CAN FINE.

4

Da yû genef dônsya.
I LIKE DANCING.

Deudhen couple

Donsya lemmyn a² vynta jŷ?
DANCE NOW WILL YOU?

7

Ymóns ŷ ow⁺talleth dônsya lemmyn.
THEY ARE STARTING TO DANCE NOW.

8

Gwell² vŷa genes bôs omma?
WOULD YOU RATHER BE HERE?

Bŷa, hep mar.
YES, OF COURSE.

So also with <u>genes</u>, <u>ganso</u>, <u>gensy</u>, <u>genen</u>, etc (see lesson 12)
So also—<u>Drôk yû genef</u>—Bad is with me (I don't like)

A gaf 'vŷ donsya <u>genes</u>?—May I dance with you?
<u>kefyth</u>—You may

SAY & TRANSLATE

Dônsya a² yllons ŷ..................

Ymá an dôns ow⁺talleth...........

Gwell yû genef eva tê.............

A² vŷa gwell genes bos trê?

....

Ny²yllyn nŷ omwaya.............

Ymá'n bagas-ŷlow ow⁺talleth cana

....

Lager²vŷa gwell genef vŷ..........

Drôk yû genef......................

33

Mŷ	re² gerdhas	have/has walked
Tŷ	re²dhêth	" " come
Êf	re²dhyscas	" " learnt/talked
Hŷ	res êth	" " gone
Nŷ	⁻re²evas	" " drunk
Whŷ	re²dhybrys	" " eaten
Ŷ	re²omdhydhanas	" " had a good time

NOTE This set cannot be used in questions or in the negative. For these cases, use the set below.

There are other ways of expressing have/has for some verbs. A useful ones is gallas (he, she, it has gone.

a²	wrugavŷ	dones	e.g.
ny2	wrussta	dysky	Did you come?
a²ny2	wruyd	mones	You did not come?
fatel²	wruk hŷ	eva	Didn't you come?
(how)	wrussyn nŷ	dyhry	How did you come?
	wrussough whŷ	donsya	
	wrussons ŷ	amma	etc.

34

NOTE As before, if you mention what you did before the "did", then this set can be used to express a statement of fact e.g. Mos__a wruga vŷ—Go I did; I went. Dybry a wrussyn nŷ—Eat we did; we ate.

The same meaning can be expressed by using mŷ, tŷ, êf, hŷ, etc with a wruk (see Lesson 5) e.g.
Mŷ a wrug amma—I kissed
Whŷ a wruk donsya—You danced
(Again, not possible as a question or in negative)
re² (a²)—too much (of)

SAY & TRANSLATE
Mŷ re evas ....
Dôs___y'n car-tân a wrussta?
....

Gwrussyn.........Na wrussyn.....
Gallas rê a vôs gansa.............
OR Ŷ re dhybrys rê a vôs..........
Hŷ re omdhydhanas................
Gallas rê a goref ganso...........
OR Êf re evas rê a goref..........
Whŷ re garas rê.................
Fatel wrussough whŷ henna?.......
Fatel wrussons dôs___?...........
Gallas hŷ medhow..............

35

PAST TENSE using was/were plus
action in -ing (see Lesson 9)

Yth esen vŷ
Yth eses
Yth esava   Ow⁴ quarŷ—playing
Yth esa hŷ   ow⁴ trŷghy—winning
Yth esen nŷ   ow⁴ tremena—passing
Yth eseugh whŷ   ow⁴ talleth—beginning
Yth esens ŷ   owth eva—drinking

NOTE For negative, use nyns instead
of yth. Nyns esên vŷ ow⁴quarŷ—I was
not playing.
For question, leave out yth. Esough
whŷ ow⁴quarŷ?—Were you playing?

trê—home   gweles—see
yn trê—at home   worteweth—at last
a-dre—away, from home defry—sure,
                           indeed.

36

SAY & TRANSLATE

Da ô genen an abaden..................

Nŷ re dhêth worteweth...............

Gweles an fyt a wrussta?............

Ny wrussyn nŷ gweles an fyt?.......

....

Stack Stevens usy ow quarŷ hedhyû?

....

Ny wrugava potya'n bêl

....

Ny wrussons ŷ trŷghŷ

Nyns esên vŷ ena.......................

Nyns esên nŷ ow quarŷ...............

Nyns esês ow quarŷ'n ta

....

Tro y'n Mês

êf—he
eef—He (emphatic)
perth—quickset hedge
lyes—many (used with sg. noun)
ke—Cornish hedge

FUTURE TIME   Refer to Lesson 10&6
Examples   Gweles devês a' vynnaf
My a' vyn gweles devês
Gweles devês a' vynnaf
My a' wra gweles devês
All mean — I will see sheep

38

SAY & TRANSLATE

Mŷ a² vyn mones y'n mês.....................................
Ny²vynnough whŷ dôs ....
An tÿak a² vyn molhethy..
A² vynnough whŷ mones ynwéth?...........................
Ŷ a²'n gweles an drê...
Nŷ a² vyn môs   a - dro..
Da²'vŷth   gensy eskynna'n bryn...............................
Mŷ, ny² vÿnnaf ....

Pandr'us y'n bellwolok? — What's on T.V.?
Brenda Wootton yma y'n bellwolok — Brenda Wootton's on T.V.

Plê ma'n paper newodhow? — Where's the newspaper?
Ymá an paper newodhow war an lur. — The paper is on the floor.

Pandr 'us y'n paper? — What's in the paper?
Travyth! — Nothing!

Pandr 'usy an fleghes ow cul? — What are the children doing?
Ymóns-ŷ y'n gwelŷ. — They are in bed.

40

(literally) war²
(figuratively) worth
by—worth
...—dres
er—yn dan⁺
ront (of)—a-vak
...nd—a-dryf (dhe)⁺
...de—ryp
...he right (of)—a-dhyghow (dhe)⁺
he left (of)—a-gleth (dhe)⁺
yn
means of—der

NOW ANSWER THESE QUESTIONS

Plê⁵' ma an ky?...............................

Pandr'usy aga³ deu⁺ ow⁺ cul war an gwelŷ-deth?...........

Pandr 'us y'n bellwolok?....................

Plê ' ma'n lyver-termyn (magazine)? ....

Us glow war'an⁺tân?..........................

Us plas war an vôs?..........................

Yû têk an⁺vowes?...........................

Yû ygor an croglennow?........................

41

GRAMMAR! agh!

An Ur/The Time

Us uryor genough-why? — Have you a watch (with you)?
Py ur yû? — What time is it?
Hanterdêth yû. — It is midday.
Hanternôs yû. — It is midnight.
Un ur yû. — It is one o'clock.
Dyw ur yû. — It is two o'clock.
So also: tŷr ur; pedêr ur; pymp ur etc. (N.B. "ur" is
  feminine)
P'ur'whrama dôs ? — When shall I come?
Dhe' naw ur. — At nine.

Quartron wosa dyw. — Quarter past two.
Quartron dhe' beder. — Quarter to four.
Ugans (mynysen) wosa whêgh. — Twenty past six.
Hanter wosa tyr. — Half past three.
Ogas êth ur. —Nearly eight.
Dêk ur poran. — Ten exactly.
Yntra naw ur ha pymp wosa naw. — Between nine and five past.

Arghadow/Imperative (Commands)

Do—Gwreugh. Don't—Na' wreugh. Let's—Gwren.
Let's not—Na' wren. Commands can be made from
most verbs by using these words, e.g. Gwreugh dos—
Come. Na' wreugh ankevy—Don't forget. Gwren mos—.
Let's go.

But here are some common commands without using the
verb DO:

Deugh—come	Lenneugh—read
Keugh—go	Danveneugh—send
Seveugh—Stop, stand	Gwerseugh—help (take dhe)
Sa ' ban—get up	(Gwereseugh dhym—help me)
Dun—let's go	But if calling for help—Harow!
Levereugh—tell	Festynneugh—hurry
Cowseugh—say	Nag ankeveugh—don't forget
Scryfeugh—write	Bedheugh war—be careful

Some Adjectives

good, better, best = da, gwell, an gwella
big, bigger, biggest = bras, brassa, an brassa
small, smaller, smallest = bŷghan, bŷghanna, an bŷghanna
bad, worse, worst = drok, gweth, an gwetha

as...as...mar^2...avel Mar'wyn avel an êrgh—White as snow
than—ages Êf yû cotha ages Myghal—He is older than Michael

Remember to put your adjective after what it is describing
(A pretty girl—A girl pretty—Moren' dêk OR Mowes têk)

RULE: Add es to number
from 5 to 9. Add yes from
10 to 20. (Change final K
to G first)

NOTE: From 20 to 200 Cornish
numbers go in scores so that
there are no separate "names"
for 30, 50, 70, 90, 110; 130 etc,
though you can use hanter cans for
50 on its own.

Nyverow/Numbers

1 onen (but with noun—un)
2 deu² (m); dyw² (f)
3 trŷ³ (m); tŷr³ (f)
4 peswar (m) peder (f)
5 pymp
6 whêgh
7 seyth
8 êth
9 naw ("now")
10 dêk ("dayk")
11 unnek
12 deudhek
13 tredhek
14 peswardek
15 pymthek   1st. kensa (1a)
16 whêtek   2nd assa (2a)
17 seytek   3rd tressa (3a)
18 êtek   4th peswera (4a)
19 nawnjek   5th pympes (5es)
20 ugans   6th wheghes (6es)
    7th seythes (7es)
    8th êthes (8es)
    9th nawes (9es)
    10th degves (10ves)

SO: 21—onen warn ugans 22—deu'warn ugans etc
30—dek warn ugans 31—unnek warn ugans etc
40—deugans 41—onen ha deugans 42—deu'ha deugans etc
50—dêk ha deugans 60—tryûgans 70—dêk ha tryugans
80—peswar-ugans 90—dek ha peswar-ugans 100—cans
101—cans hag onen (etc up to 120) 120—whêgh-ugans
121—whegh-ugans hag onen 140—seyth ugans 160—êth-ugans
180—naw-ugans 200—deucans 300—tryhans 400—peswar cans
500—pymp cans etc 1000—mŷl¹ 2000—dyw¹vŷl¹ 3000—tremmŷl¹
4000—peder mŷl¹ 1,000,000—mŷlvŷl¹ 2,000,000—dyw¹vylvŷl¹
3,000,000—tŷr¹mylvŷl¹ £1,000—mŷl¹buns
The Good News—You don't use plurals after a number.
12 eggs—deudhek oy
The Bad News—If your number is made up of more than one
part (e.g.) onen warn ugans—(21) and you use it with a noun
(e.g. 21 miles) you mention the noun after the first part of
the number—21 miles—un myldŷr warn ugans
324 miles—tryhans myldŷr ha peswar warn ugans
NOTE: After deu' & dyw', soft mutation—deu'bynta—2 pints
After trŷ'& tŷr', spirant mutation—trŷ'fynta—3 pints

Prepositions

Be ready for certain differences in the use of prepositions.
You'll get this in any language. Here are some common ones:

Don't be angry with me—Na²wreugh serry orthyf ("at me")
Kiss me—Amdhym (kiss "to me")
He dodged the tackle—Ef a'wruk scusy rag an'dhalghen (dodged "for").
Fill it with water—Gwra ŷ'lenwel a'dhowr ("of" water)
Have you heard from George?—Clewes gans Jory a'wrussys?
("with"George)
He's grumbling about the price—Ymá ow'crothval war'an cost.
("on" the cost)
NOTE: Don't use gans for "with" in "talk with".
My a garsa kewsel dhyso-jŷ—I'd like to speak to you/with you.
but My a garsa kewsel genes—I'd like to speak on your behalf
I must etc., is expressed by rês yû dhe'—I must go: Rês yû dhym
môs . To look after—gwytha war¹
Prepositions combine with pronouns as follows:

gans—with	dhe²—to	worth—to, at,	rak—for	war²—on	a²—of
genef	dhym	worthyf	ragof	warnaf	ahanaf
genes	dhys	worthys	ragos	warnas	ahanas
ganso	dhodho	worto	ragtho	warnodho	anodho
gensy	dhedhy	worty	rygthy	warnedhy	anedhy
genen	dhyn	worthyn	ragon	warnan	ahanan
genough	dheugh	worthough	ragough	warnough	ahanough
gansa	dhedha	worta	ragtha	warnedha	anedha

Possessions: An cota-na yu dhyso-jŷ—That coat is yours (to you).

Mutation

Mutation (or change) of the first letter in certain circumstances is a feature of all Celtic languages. It takes time to get used to, so don't be frightened of making mistakes. You'll still be understood.

If the normal state of the first letter of a word is regarded as State 1, then the softening of this letter is called State 2, the "breathing" of it, State 3, the hardening of it, State 4. There is also a mixed State 5. The affected letters are tabulated below:

STATE 1	STATE 2	STATE 3	STATE 4	STATE 5
b	v	no change	p	f or v
c, k	g	h	no change	no change
ch	j	no change	"	"
d	dh	"	t	t
f	pron. v but sp. "f"	"	no change	no change
g	sometimes w or left out	"	c,k	h
gw	w	"	qu	wh or w
m	v	"	no change	no change
p	b	f	"	f or v
qu	gw	wh	"	no change
s	pron 'z' but sp . 's'	no change	"	"
t	d	th	"	"

<u>Various words</u> cause a following first letter to change to state 2 Commonest are: <u>dhe</u>²—(to) Mary—<u>Marŷa</u>; to Mary—dhe²Varŷa
<u>pur</u>²(very) da—good; <u>pur²dha</u>—very good
<u>mar</u>²(as/so) <u>kether</u>—pretty; mar²gether—as pretty
(so pretty);ŷ (his) <u>pen</u> (head);ŷ ben—his head
<u>na</u>²(not) <u>gwreugh</u>—do; na²wreugh—do not
<u>deu</u>²; dyw²(2) (as in lesson 6)

<u>an</u> (the) also causes State 2 with a feminine word (if singular)
<u>mowes</u>...an²vowes (but—mowysy—girls..<u>an mowysy</u>—the girls)
<u>an</u> (the) also causes State 2 with the plural of masculine words
if they refer to people: <u>tus</u>—men, an²dus—the men
This rule also applies to <u>un</u>—one
<u>Finally</u> , in this State 2, any feminine (singular) or masculine
(plural),(and referring to people) nouns will cause softening
of a following adjective: <u>benen</u>—woman <u>brâs</u>—big ; benen²vras—
big woman. <u>gwŷthoryon</u>—workmen <u>da</u>—good; gwŷthoryon²dha—
good workmen.

The commonest causes of State 3 are;

<u>trŷ</u>³—three <u>puns</u>—pound; trŷ³funs—three pounds
<u>tŷr</u>³—three (f) <u>pluven</u>—feather; Tŷr³Fluven—Three Feathers.
<u>hŷ</u>³—her <u>tâs</u>—father; hŷ³thas—her father
<u>ow</u>³—my car—<u>friend</u>; ow³har—my friend
<u>aga</u>³—their <u>torn</u>—turn; aga³thorn—their turn

When expressing actions ending in -ing (coming, going etc)
you put ow before the verb, and use State 4.
dones—to come ow⁺tones—coming
bryjyon—to boil ow⁺pryjyon—boiling etc.

State 5 is used with p'ur'? (when). P'ur'whreugh-whŷ mos?—
When do you go? And with Prak y (why?)...see below: Other
complications can safely be left for more advanced study.

NOTE: Don't confuse pur (very: State 2) with p'ur (when:
State 5)

Words Used to Introduce Questions

US? = Is there? are there? Answer = Us—yes, there is/are—
    Nag us—no there isn't/aren't
    Us coref omma? = Is there (any) beer here?
    Ūs.=Yes, there is. Nag us = No there isn't.
Usy an? = Is the...? Is...? where the thing or person
    referred to is definite (must also be a question of place
    or position)
    Usy agas tas yn-chŷ? = Is your father in?
    Usy an lêth y'n rewgell? = Is the milk in the fridge?
    Answer = Usy. Nag usy.
Plê? = Where? Plê' ma'n gwaya mŷr? = Where is the cinema?'
A'blê? = Where from? A bleth esough-whŷ ow tos? =
                Where are you coming from?
Fatel? = How? Fatel'esough-whŷ ow cul? = How are you doing?
Pandr'a'? = What? Pandr'a' vynnough-whŷ cafos? = What'll you have?
P'ur5? = When? P'ur' fyth êf parys? = When will it be ready?
prag y5? = Why? Prag y'whrava hy'hasa? = Why does he dislike her?
Prag na'? = Why not? Prag na'wreugh-whŷ gortos? = Why don't you stay?
Pes, pygemmys? = How much/many? Pygemmys a' vynough-whŷ prena?
    How much (many) will you buy? Pes myldyr yû? = How many miles is it?
Pyû? = Who? Pyû yu an den ,na? Who is that man? Pyû yua? Who is it?
    Pyû a vyn dos? Who is going to come? P'yûa? What is it? What's
    up?

NOTE: When is is used for describing or identifying a person
    or thing, use yû (not us)
    Pandr'yû henna? What is that?
    Pygemmys hês yû? How long is it?
    Pell yûa? Is it far?

This & That

This man—an den ma   That man—an den na
This girl—an'voren ma That girl—an'voren na.
These—an rê ma Those—an rê na

This one—hemma (m) homma (f) That one—henna (m) honna (f)
This is—hem yû (m) hom yû (f) That is—hen yû (m) hon yû (f)

THE CORNISH SENTENCE

1 Being

BEING With reference to <u>identity</u> or <u>description</u>:
For statement of FACT, use...

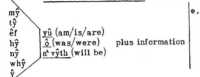

mŷ		e.g. Mŷ yû squŷth
tŷ		I am tired;
êf	yû (am/is/are)	Êf o pŷs da
hŷ	ô (was/were) plus information	He was pleased;
nŷ	a⋅vŷth (will be)	Nŷ a⋅vŷth ledhys
whŷ		We'll be killed
ŷ		

OR: State your information and add....

Present	Past	Future
oma	ena/en vy	vydhaf-vŷ
osta	esta	voydhyth
yûa	ova	vytha
yûŷ	o hŷ	vythŷ
on nŷ	en nŷ	vydhyn nŷ
ough whŷ	eugh whŷ	vydhough whŷ
yns ŷ	ens ŷ	vydhons ŷ

e.g. Squŷth ôma—I'm tired
Pŷs da ôva—He was pleased
Ledhys⋅vydhyn-nŷ—We'll be killed

For statements of NON-FACT, use...

Present	Past	Future
Nyns oma	Nyns ena	Ny⋅vydhaf-vŷ
nyns osta	nyns esta	ny⋅vydhyth
nyns yûa	nyns ova	ny⋅vytha
nyns yûŷ	nyns ô hŷ	ny⋅vythŷ
nyns on nŷ	nyns en nŷ	ny⋅vydhyn nŷ
nyns ough whŷ	nyns eugh-whŷ	nŷ⋅vydhough whŷ
nyns yns ŷ	nyns ens ŷ	ny⋅vydhons ŷ

e.g. Nyns oma parys—I'm not ready Ny⋅vytha da lowr—
It won't be good enough.

For questions, use...

Present	Past	Future
oma	ena	a⋅vydhaf-vŷ
osta	esta	a⋅vydhyth
yûa	ova	a⋅vytha
yûŷ	ô hŷ	a⋅vythŷ
on nŷ	en nŷ	a⋅vydhyn nŷ
ough whŷ	eugh whŷ	a⋅vydhough whŷ
yns ŷ	ens ŷ	a⋅vydhons ŷ

(placing the information either side of
the verb)

e.g. Parys osta? OR Osta parys?—Are you ready?
For answers: Use Of; nag of. Yû, nag yû. On, nag on.
Ough, nag ough . Yns, nag yns. En, nag en. O, nag o.
En, nag en. Eugh, nag eugh. Ens, nag ens. Bydhaf,
na⋅vydhaf. Bŷth, na⋅vŷth. Bydhyn, na⋅vydhyn. Bydhough,
na⋅vydhough. Bydhons, na⋅vydhons.

2 Being

BEING With reference to place or continuous action.
For statements of Fact, use...

Present	Past	
Yth esof. vŷ	Yth esen, vŷ	Use future set as in
Yth esos jŷ	Yth. eses. vŷ	section one
Ymava	Yth esa, ga	
Ymá ,hŷ	Yth esa hŷ	plus information on
Yth eson nŷ	Yth esen nŷ	place OR plus ow⁴
Yth esough	Yth eseugh	and verb
whŷ	whŷ	
Ymóns ŷ	Yth esens ŷ	

e.g. Yth esên·vŷ ow'parusy hansel—I was getting
breakfast ready. Ymons–ŷ y'n gegyn—They're in
the kitchen. Êf a vŷth yn Kertsk—He'll be in Exeter.

For statements of NON-FACT, use

Present	Past	Future
Nyns esof vŷ	Nyns esen vy	As in section
Nyns esos jŷ	Nyns eses vŷ	one
Nyns usy ef	Nyns esa vâ	
Nyns usy hŷ	Nyns esa hŷ	
Nyns eson nŷ	Nyns esen nŷ	
Nyns esough	Nyns eseugh	
whŷ	whŷ	
Nyns esons ŷ	Nyns esens ŷ	

For QUESTIONS, use...set as in NON-FACT but without
the word nyns e.g. Yn Stret an Grows usy êf?—In Cross
Street is it? Ow'cwytha esens··y?—Working were they?

For ANSWERS, use...Esof, nag esof, Esos, nag esos.
Usy, nag usy. Eson, nag eson. Esough, nag esough,
Esons, nag esons. Esen, nag esen. Esa, nag esa. Esen,
nag esen, Eseugh, nag eseugh, Esens, nag esens

3 Actions

ACTIONS For continuous actions use set 2, with ow⁴. So...
Dos—to come; Yth esof-vŷ ow'tos—I'm coming.
Otherwise, the simplest way of expressing an action is to
use the verb to do (gul) with the verb of your action. So...

A. Statement of FACT:

Mŷ	a²wruk (I did)	cafos (find)	
Tŷ		gweles (see)	
Ef		danvon (send)	plus action
Hŷ	a²wra (do, does)	prena (buy)	
Nŷ	(will do)	etc	
Whŷ	a²vyn (will do)		
Ŷ			

B. NON-FACT & QUESTION :

Ny² (not)	wraf vŷ	wrugavŷ	vynnaf· vŷ	
	wrêta	wrussta	vynnyth	
A (for question)	wrava	wruga	vyn êf	
	wra· hŷ	wruk hŷ	vyn hŷ	e.g.
A²ny²(neg. quest.)	wren nŷ	wrussyn nŷ	vynnyn nŷ	Ny²wraf.vŷ megy—I don't smoke
	wreugh whŷ	wrussough whŷ	vynnough whŷ	A wrêta dônsya?—Do you dance?
	wrons ŷ	wrussons ŷ	vynnons ŷ	A ny²vynnons ŷ dones?—Won't
				they come?

NOTE: Mŷ, tŷ, êf, hŷ, Nŷ, whŷ, ŷ or nouns can be put before
ny: e.g. Mŷ ny'vynnaf kewsel Sawsnek—I won't speak English.

ANSWERS: Gwraf, na²wraf. Gwra, na²wra. Gwren, na²wren.
Gwreugh, na²wreugh. Gwrons, na²wrons. Gwruk, na²wruk,
Gwrussyn, na²wrussyn. Gwrussough, na²wrussough. Gwrussons,
na²wrussons. Mynnaf, na²vynnaf. Myn, na²vyn. Mynnyn, na²
vynnyn. Mynnough, na²vynnough. Mynnons, na²vynnons.

4 Liking & Wishing

mŷ			dônsya (dance)
tŷ			gwedren aᵗwyn (glass of wine)
êf	aᵗgar (like, likes)		mones trê (go home)
hŷ			etc.
nŷ	aᵗgarsa (would like)		
whŷ			
ŷ			

	like, likes	would like	
Ny² (not)	garaf vŷ	garsen vŷ	
	geryth	garses jŷ	
A² (questions)	gar êf	garsava	
	gar hŷ	garsa hŷ	plus action
Aᵗny² (neg quest.)	geryn nŷ	garsen nŷ	
	gerough whŷ	garseugh whŷ	
	garons ŷ	garsens ŷ	

5 Wanting

WANTING (mynnes: to want)

mŷ		
tŷ		
êf	aᵗ vyn (want; wants)	plus
hŷ	aᵗvynna (wanted)	action
nŷ	aᵗvynsa (would want)	
whŷ		
ŷ		

Ny² (not)	vynnaf vŷ	vynnen vŷ	vynsen vŷ	
	vynta jŷ	vynnes jŷ	vynses ta	
A² (questions)	vyn êf	vynnava	vynsava	
	vyn hŷ	vynna hŷ	vynsa hŷ	
A ny² (neg. quest.)	vynnyn ʉŷ	vynnen nŷ	vynsen nŷ	
	vynnough whŷ	vynneugh whŷ	vynseugh whŷ	
	vynnons ŷ	vynnens ŷ	vynsens ŷ	

ANSWERS: Mynnaf, naᵗvynnaf etc.

6 Being Able

BEING ABLE: (gallos: to be able)

mŷ		
tŷ		
êf	aᵗŷl (can)	
hŷ	aᵗylly (could)	plus action
nŷ	aᵗalsa (might)	
whŷ		
ŷ		

A² (questions)	allaf vŷ	yllyn vŷ	alsen vŷ	
	ylta jŷ	ylles jŷ	alses jŷ	
Ny² (negative)	yl êf	ylly êf	alsa êf	
	yl hŷ	ylly hŷ	alsa hŷ	
A ny² (neg. quest.)	yllyn nŷ	yllyn nŷ	alsen nŷ	
	yllough whŷ	ylleugh whŷ	alseugh whŷ	
	yllons ŷ	yllens ŷ	alsens ŷ	

ANSWERS: Gallaf, naᵗallaf. Gyllyn, naᵗyllyn.
Galsen, naᵗalsen etc.

7 Possession

ow³	my	me	e.g: I like him—Mŷ aᵗwra ŷᵗgara
dha²	your	you	(lit: I do his like)
y²	his	him	I don't like him—Nyᵗwraf ŷᵗgara
hŷ³	her	her	(lit. I don't his like)
agan	our	us	I couldn't see them—Nyᵗyllyn agaᵗ
agas	your	you	gweles (lit. I could not their see)
aga³	their	them	

NOTE: These cause mutations indicated by numbers.

My coat—Ow³hota   This coat is mine—An cota-ma yû dhymmo-vŷ*
*See under PREPOSITIONS
Whose is...?   Dheᵗbyû yû...?

VOCABULARY
English·· Kernewek

A

a—usually left out in Cornish
able: to be able—gallos, vb
above—a-ûgh (as rak), prep
accept—degmeres, vb
ache—pystyga, vb; glôs, fn
across—a-drus (as rak), prep & adv
address—trygva, fn; scryva trygva
war², vb
aeroplane—jyn nyja, fn
after—warlergh, prep & adv; war ow
lergh after me (of time); wosa, prep,
wosa hanter ur after half an hour
agree (with)—unverhé(gans), vb
all—all the people—an dus oll; all the
men—pup dên oll; at·all—gêr vyth—
no ward at all; ný wòn man—I don't
know at all
alright—Is he alright now—Da lowr yû
lemmyn?; Is it alright to go without
permission?—Ewn yû mones hep
amyas?
also—ynwéth, adv
always—pupprýs, adv
and—ha(g), conj
angry—serrys, adj
animal—eneval, mn
answer—gorthyby, vb; gorthyp, mn
any—anything—neppyth, prn; (with
neg—travyth); anywhere—yn levyth,
adv; anyone—neboren, prn; (with
neg—denvyth); anyway—'fors fatel vo
apron—raglen, fn
arm—bregh, fn
at—at Bodmin—dhe'Vodmenêgh; at
Truro—yn Truro; at six o'clock—
dhe'whêgh ur; at|last—worteweth);
adv.
aunt—modryp; fn
awake—dyfun; adj
away—(position) a-vês, adv; (motion)
dhe-vês, adv
awful—uthek, adj

B

baby—baban, mn
back—(of body) keyn, mn; (of hand,
house, page, etc.) kýl, mn; back—
yn-tro, adv.
bacon—bakken, mn
bad—drŏk, adj
bake—pobas, vb
basket—canstel, fn
be—bôs, vb
beach—trêth, mn
beautiful—têk, adj
bed—gwely, mn

---

bedroom—chambour, mn
beer—coref, mn
before the Town Hall—a-rak
Lýs an'Drêf; before November—kens
es Mýs Dû; before he came—kens del¹
dhéth; before long—kens pell
behind—a-dryf (prep), + dhe'with prn
believe—crysy, vb; I don't believe it—
Ny'n crysaf, I don't believe you—
Ný'grysaf dhys
bell—clŏgh, fn
belly—tor, fn
below—a-ýs, prep; (as rak)
bent—cam, adj
better—gwell, adj; gwellhé, vb
between—yntra, prep; (ynter before
vowels)
big—brâs, adj
bigger—brassa, adj
biggest—an brassa, adj
bird—edhen, mn
black—du, adj
blanket—len-gwely, fn
blouse—crýs, mn
boil—bryjyon, vb;|whejalen, fn
bone—ascorn, mn
book—lyver, mn
boot—botasen, fn
boy—maw, mn
bra—brongolm, mn
bread—bara, mn; bread & butter—bara'
manyn
break—terry, vb
breakfast—hansel, mn
bridge—pons, mn
bring—drý, vb
broad—ledan, adj
brother—broder, mn
brown—dark b—gorm, adj; light b—
gell, adj
bucket—kelorn, mn
building—dreghevyans, mn
burn—lesky, vb
bus—kyttryn, mn; pl-yow
busy—bysy, adj
but—mes, conj
butter—amanyn, mn
by—a book by James Conolly—lyver
gans James Conolly; I won by running—
Mý a fethas ow ponya; a house by the
river—chy ryp an avon; by now—
erbýn an ur ma
buy—prena, vb; (coll. perna)

C

cake—têsen, fn
call—gelwel, vb; galow, mn
cap—cappa, mn
capitalist—kevalavor, mn
car—car-tân, mn

---

care(for)—look after—gwytha war², vb
I don't care—ny'm dur, vb
carry—degy, vb
castle—castel, fn
cat—cath, fn
catch—bagha, vb
celebrate—gŏlya, vb
century—cansvledhen, fn
chair—cadar, fn
change—nowys, vb & mn; (small)
change, cash—mona, mn
chapel—chapel, fn
cheap—a'vargen da
cheese—kês, mn
chemist—(pharmacist)—ferellyth, mn
ch's shop ferellý, mn; (scientist)—
kymyor, mn
child—flŏgh, mn
chips—(potato ch., crisps)—cressygow
mpln. (fried ch.)—asclas, mn
chipshop—asclattý, mn
cigarette—sygaryk, mn
cinema—gwaya myr. mn
city—kêr, fn
class—(in school)—dosparth, mn
(in society)—rencas, fn; working
class—rencas-ober
clean—glân, adj
clear—(transperent)—ylyn, adj;
(obvious)—clêr, adj
climb—crambla, vb
clock—clok, mn
close—degea, vb
closed—degés, adj
cloud—comolen, fn
coal—glow, mn
coat—cota, mn; overcoat—cota-brâs;
raincoat—cota-stanch
coffee—cafe, mn; instant c.—cafe-scon
cold—yeyn, adj
coldness—yeynder, mn
come—dôs, vb
comfortable—attés, adj; Are you c.?—
Attés ôs? Is the chair c.?—Attés
dhys yû'n'gadar?
cornish—kernewek, adj; C. language—
Kernewek, mn; Cornishman—Kernow
mn; Cornishwoman—Kerwomes, fn
count—nyvera, vb
country—pow, mn
county—conteth, mn
cow—bûgh, fn
cow's house—bowjý, mn
cream—dêhen, mn; ice-cream—dêhen-
rew
cup—hanaf, mn; a cup of tea
cupboard—ámary, mn
cupful—hanafas, fn
cut—treghy, vb
cider—cyder, mn

D

dance—dônsya, vb; dôns, mn
dark—tewl, adj
darkness—tewlder, mn
dart—sêthen, fn
dear—ker, adj; my dear-to child—
  'genesyk; to spouse, sweetheart—
  'vŷghan (in general) 'sôs
defeat—fetha, vb; fethans, mn
difficult—anês, adj
dinner—(at home)—lŷ, mn; (at work)—
  crowst, mn
dirty—plôs, adj
dish—scudel, fn
do—gul, vb
dog—kŷ, mn
door—darras, mn
dress—(costume) gwysk, fn, (frock)—
  pows, fn; gwysca, vb; d. oneself—
  omwysca, vb
drink—eva, vb; (d. liquor)—dewassa, vb
  las, mn; liquor dewas, mn
drive—lewyas, vb
drop—bera, vb
drunk—medhow, adj
dry—segha, vb; sêgh, adj
dust—pon, mn

E

each—pup, adj
ear—scovarn, fn
early—a-var, adv
earth—dôr, mn; The E.—An Nôr
east—howldhrevel, mn
easy—ês, adj
eat—dybry, vb
egg—oy, mn
electricity—tredan, mn
empty—gwak, adj
end—deweth, mn
engage—gwystla. vb vb
english—sawsnek, adj; E. language—
  Sawsnek, mn; Englishman—Saws, mn
  Englishwoman—Sawsnes, fn
enjoy—cafos blas war², vb; e. oneself
  —omdhydhana, vb
evening—androw, mn
every—pup, adj
everything—puptra, prn(f)
excellent—bryntyn, adj
except—marnas, ma's, prep
expect—desevos, vb
expensive—druth/ker, adj
eye—lagas, mn

F

face—enep, fn
fair—(light coloured)—gwyn, adj;
  (beautiful)—têk, adj; (right)—eun,
  adj
fall—côdha, vb
far—pell, adj
farm —bargen-tŷr, mn
fast—snell, adj
fat—berryk, adj; tew, adj

father—tâs, mn
fear—perthy own a², vb; own, mn
feel—feel the cold—clewes an yeynder;
  feel ill—omglewes claf
field—(general)—park, mn; (pasture)—
  prâs, mn; (arable, for game)—gwêl,
  mn
fill—lenwel, vb
film—at cinema—gwaya-mŷr, mn; for
  camera—snod, mn
find—cafos, vb
fine—brâf, adj
finger—bys, mn
finish—gorfenna, vb; (complete)—
  cowlwul, vb
fish—pysk, mn; p yskessa, vb
floor—lur, mn
flower—blejen, fn; blejewa, vb
fog—newl, mn
food—bôs, mn
foot—trôs, fn
for—rak, prep
forest—côswŷk, fn
fortnight—dyw seythen, fn; in a f's
  time—hedhyu yn dan seythen
free—rŷth, adj; (free of charge)—
  dydâl, adj
fresh—(new)—noweth, adj; (of food,
  milk, etc)—cro, adj;(of weather)—
  clôr, adj
frock—pows, fn
fruit—fruyth, mn
fry—frŷa, vb
full—lun, adj
funny—wharthus, adj
furniture—gutrolow, mpln

G

game—gwarŷ, mn; (match—abaden, fn
garden—lowarth, fn
garment—dyllas, mn
gate—yet, mn
get—cafos, vb; get onto bus—eskynna
  yn kettryn; get off train—dyeskynna a
  drên; get up—sevel yn ban; get
  married—prŷosa, vb; get off! get out!
  —kê dhe gerdhes!
girl—mowes, fn; (young woman, maid)
  —moren, fn
give—rŷ, vb; give in(to)—omrŷ(dhe)
glad—lowen, adj
glove—manek, fn
go—mos, vb
gone—gyllys, adj
good—(of people)—mâs, adj; (generally)
  —da, adj
goodbye—Dew genes
grandfather—tâs-wyn, mn
grandmother—mam-wyn, fn

grass—gwels, fn
grate—maglen-clân, fn
great—mûr, adj
green—gwer, adj; glâs, adj
grocer—spŷsor, mn
grow—tevy, vb

H

hair—(of head) gols, mn; (of body)
  blew, mn

half—hanter, mn
halfpenny—demma, mn
hall—hêl, mn; Town Hall—Lŷs an Drêf,
  mn; County Hall—Lŷs an Pou
hand—luf, fn; h. of clock—nasweth, fn
hard—cales, adj
hat—hot, mn
hate—casa, vb
have—I have—ymá genef (see Grammar)
he—êf, prn
head—pen, mn
health—yeghes, mn
healthy—yagh, adj
hear—clewes, vb
heart—colon, fn
heavy—pôs, adj
hedge—Cornish h.,—kê, mn; h. of
  bushes—perth, mn
help—gweres, mn; gul gweres dhe², vb
  Help!—Harow!
hen—yar, fn
here—omma, adv; from here—glemma, adv
high—ûghel, adj; It's high time to—Prŷs
  mur yu
hill—bryn, mn; brê, fn
holidays—gôlyow, fpln
home—trê, fn; at h.—yn trê, adv; from
  h.—a-drê, adv; h. work—scolober, mn;
  omrewleth, fn
honey—mêl, mn
hope—gwaytans, mn; I hope...—ymá
  gwaytyans dlym...
horse—margh, mn
hospital—clavjy, mn
hot—pôth, adj
hotel—gwestŷ, mn
hour—ur, fn
house—chŷ, fn
hundred—cans, mn
hurry—festyna, vb; h. up!—festyn!
husband—gour, mn

I

I—mŷ, mn
ice—rew, mn
ill—claf, adj
illness—cleves, mn
important—pôsek, adj; bysy, adj
in—yn; in time—a-dermyn, adv
interesting—a-vern, adj; very i.—
  mur ŷ lês
invitation—kyfvewyans, mn
island—enys, fn
it—êf, m prn; hŷ, f prn

J

jacket—jerkyn, mn
jail—pryson, mn
jam—kyfŷth, mn
journey—vyach, mn
jug—podyk, mn
jump—lam, mn; lemmel, vb

K

keep—gwytha, vb
kettle—caltor /chek, fn

50

kick—pot, mn; potya, vb
kind—cuf, adj; whêk, adj
kitchen—kegyn, fn
knife—collel, fn
know—(k. a fact)—godhvos, vb; (k. a person)—aswonvos, vb

L

lake—lôgh, fn
lamb—ôn, fn
lame—clof, adj
land—tŷr, mn
language—yêth, fn
last—dewetha, adj; l. week—an seythen usy tremenys; at l.—worteu-eth, adv; last night—n'ewer, adv
late—dewedhes, adj; a'-dhewedhes, adv
laugh—wharth, mn; wherthyn, vb
lean—pôsa, vb
learn—dysky, vb; dysky Kernewek—learning Cornish
least—lŷha, adj
leave—gasa, vb; (depart)—vodya, vb
left—cleth, adj; on the left—a-gleth, adv
leg—gar, fn
less—lê, adj
let—gasa, vb; to let a flat—gorra ranjŷ, vb
letter—lyther, mn; (of alphabet—lytheren, fn
lid—gorher, mn
lie down—growedha, vb
life—bewnans, mn
light—golow, mn; (lamp)—lugarn, mn; electric light—lugarn tredan
light—(in colour)—clêr, adj; gwyn, adj (in weight)—scaf, adj
like—cara, vb; I like it very much—mur y plêk dhym
like—hevel, adj; I like them—hevel worta
list—rôl, fn
live—(be alive)—bewa, vb; (dwell)—tryga, vb
loaf—torth, fn
lonely—(of person)—dygoweth, adj; (of place)—unyk, adj
long—hŷr, adj
look (at)—mŷras (worth), vb; l. after—gwytha war²; You look well—Ymá golok dha warnas
lose—kelly, vb
love—(affection)—kerensa, fn; (romantic love—sergh, fn; cara, vb; (term of endearment)—vŷghan, m&fn; whegen, fn; whegyn, pl
lovely—têk, adj; gwyn, adj

M

machine—jyn, mn
make—gwruthyl, vb
man—dên, mn
many—lŷes, adj (t sg) as many as—kemmys...ha (def with vb)
map—mappa, fn
market—marghas, fn
marry—demedhy, vb
meat—kŷk, mn

menu—rôl-bos, mn
message—negys, mn
middle—crês, mn
mile—myldŷr, mn
milk—lêth, mn
minute—mynysen, fn
miss—miss opportunity—kelly spâs; miss target—fyllel costen; miss our friends—yeuny warlergh agan cowetha
mist—lewgh, mn
mix—kemysky, vb
money—arghans, mn
month—mŷs, mn
moon—lôr, fn
more—moy, mn
morning—myttyn, mn
most—(an) moyha, adj; m. of the people—ran vrassa'n dus
mother—mam, fn
mountain—meneth (but in Kernow use bryn or carn)
mouth—ganow, mn
move—gwaya, vb; m. oneself—omwaya, vb
much—mur a²; as much...as—kemmys ...ha/del² vb
must—you must—nês yû dhys
my—ow³, 'm (after vowels)

N

naked—nôth, fn
name—hanow, mn
narrow—cul, adj; ŷn, adj
nasty—casadow, adj
nation—kênethel, fn
national—kênethlek, adj; the national movement—omsaf an gênethel
nationalist—kênethlor, mn
naughty—drôk, adj
neck—conna, mn
new—noweth, adj; brand new—noweth-flam, adj
news—newodhow, mpln
nice—(of people)—whêk, caradou, adj; (of things)—gay, adj
nickers—lavrak-bŷghan, mn
night—nôs, fn; last night—'newer, adv; night before last—dêgensenôs, adv; tonight—haneth, adv
no—as answer to question—not generally expressed (see grammar) In agreement—Nâ
north—Cleth, mn
nose—trôn, mn
not—ny, vb prt; nyns(before vowels in môs & bôs)
nothing—netra, f prn; nothing at all—netra man
now—lemmyn, adv; y'n ur ma
nurse—clavyjor, mn; clavyjores, fn

O

o'clock—ur, fn
of—a², prep; (often not expressed)—gwyrryow'n weryn—the rights of the ordinary people
office—sodhva, fn
oil—olew, mn
old—côth, adj

on—war², prep; on fire—gans tân
once—unwyth, adv; at once—war nuk
one—ôñen, prn; huny, prn; (after an, pes?, lŷes, pup etc); un, num a adj
only—unsel, adj; hepken, adv; I can only see...—Ny welaf ma's...
open—ygor, adj; ygery, adv
or—bo, conj
orange—owraval
other—(beforen) kên, adj; (after)—ara,(adj pl evêl)
our—agan, a'n, prn
over—dres, prep

P

pack—pack the trunk—lenwel an sawgh; pack my things—sawghya'm taclow
pain—(physical)—galar, mn; (mental)—galarow, mpln
pants—lavrak-bŷghan, mn
paper—paper, mn; paper newodhou, mn
parents—(coll.) his parents—ŷ dus
park—park, mn; kewya, vb; car park—cargen, fn
party—feast, celebration—gwlêth, fn; political party—strollas, mn
pass—(go by)—tremena, vb; (pass by hand)—hedhes, vb; pass exam—sowynny yn apposyans
pasty—hogen, fn
path—hens, mn
pavement—cauns, mn
pay—to pay nim for the beer—tylly, vb dhodho'n coref; yaber, fn;
pen—scryvel, fn; quill p.—pluven, fn
penalty—penans, mn
penny—deneren, fn; (after numerals)—dynar, mn
perhaps—martesen, adv
person—person, mn
picture—pyctur, mn
pig—hogh, mn
pillow—pluvak, fn
pint—pŷnta, mn
place—(town, village, etc)—tyller, mn; (in general)—le, mn
plate—plâs, mn
platform—(in station)—eskynlur, mn
play—gwarŷ, vb; gwarŷ-mŷr, mn
pleased—pŷs da, adj; if you please—mar plêk
pocket—poket, mn
policeman—kefnysor, mn; plain-clothes,policeman—sarfor, mn
pop—(soft drink)—hothlas, mn
poor—boghosek, mn
post—(pole, stake)—pul, mn; (mail) post, mn
postman—lytherwas, mn
post office—lytherjy, mn; sub p.o.—lytherva, fn
potato—dôral, mn
prefer—she prefers—gwell yû gensy
prepare—(make ready)—parusy, vb; prepare food—darbary bûs
pretty—têk, adj
price—prŷs, mn
programme—(T.V.,Radio)—towlen, fn (of society, movement)—raglyen, fn
promise—dedhewys, fn; dedhewy, vb
proud—gothys/prowt, adj
pub—dewottŷ, mn

51

pull—tenna, vb
pump—ryboul, mn
put—gorra, vb

Q

quarrel—kédryn, mn; kedrynya, vb
quarter—quartron, mn
question—govyn, mn
queue—lost, mn; losta, vb
quiet—cosel, adj
quite—(completely)—glàn, adj

R

radio—radyo, mn
rain—glaw, mn; It's raining—Glaw a wra
raise—dreghevel, sevel, vb
reach—(stretch out for)—hedhes, vb; (arrive at)—drehedhes, vb
read—lenna, vb
ready—parys, adj
receive—degemeres, vb
recognize—aswon, vb
record—(memorial)—covath, fn; (disc) —sonblas, mn; covatha, vb; (on tape, disc)—soncryva, vb
recover—(get better)—gwella, vb; (get back)—dascafos, vb
red—cough, adj; ruth, adj
remember—(bear in mind)—perthy cof a², (recall)—I remember...—Ymâ cof dhym...
rest—powes, mn &vb
rest—(remainder)—remenant, mn
return—(come back)—dewheles, vb; (give back)—dascor, vb; (send back) —danvon yn-trô, vb
rich—kevothak, adj
right—(not left)—dyghow, adj; on the right—a'dhyghow, adv; correct—ewn, adj; (privilege, liberty)—gwŷr, mn; ewnder, mn
ring—seny, vb
ring—kelgh, mn; finger r.—bysow, mn
river—avon, fn
road—forth, fn
room—stevel, mn; Is there any room?—Us la vyth?
rose—rosen, fn
rough—garow, adj
run—(of living things)—ponya, vb; (off machines)—môs, vb; (generally):a —resek, vb

S

sad—tryst, adj
saint—sans, mn; (as title)—Synt, mn; Synta, fn
salmon—èok, mn
salt—holan, mn; sal, adj
sand—tewas, fn
sauce—sows, fn
say—leverel, vb
school—scol, fn
screen—(shelter)—sken, fn; (for film etc)—scram, mn

sea—mor, mn
second—êlyas, fn; second, num adj
see—gweles, vb
sell—gwertha, vb
sermon—pregoth, mn
she—hŷ, prn
sheep—davas, fn
shilling—sols, mn
shoe—eskys, mn
shop—gwerthjy, mn
short—ber, adj
shorts—lavvak-ber, mn
shovel—pàl, fn
show—dysquedhes, vb; stage show—gwary-mŷr, mn; agricultural show—fêr gonys-tŷr, fn
shut—degea, vb; degés, adj
side—(of person, ship, etc)—tenewan, mn; (direction)—tu, mn; by the side of—ryp, prep
silver—arghans, mn
sing—cana, vb
singer—canor, mn; canores, vb
sink—new, mn; sedhy, vb
sister—whoer, fn
sit—esedha, v; sitting down—a-eseth, adj
skin—croghen, fn
skirt—losten, fn; mini-skirt—lostennyk, fn
sky—ebren, fn
sleep—cusca, vb
slow—(of movement)—lent, adj;
small—bŷghan, adj
smile—mynwharth, mn; mynwherthyn, vb
snob—craghor, mn; craghores, fn
snow—ergh, mn; It's snowing—Ergh a wra
so—ythe, conj; (like this)—yndella, adv; (like that)—yn delma, adv
soap—seban, mn
sock—pawgen, fn
sofa—gwely-dêth, mn
someone—nebonen, prn
something—neppyth, prn
sometimes—trawythyow, adv
somewhere—le kyn fê, adv
song—cân, fn
soup—cowl, mn
speak—cows, vb
special—arbennek, adj
spirit—spyrys, mn; (drink)—gwrŷas, mn
split—fals, fn
spoon—lô, fn
stair—deres, mn
start—dalleth, mn & vb
station—railways—gorsaf, mn; bus station—kettrŷnjŷ, mn; police station—kefnyttŷ, mn
stay—(wait)—gortos, vb; (lodge)—godryga, vb
stone—mên, mn
story—whethel, mn
street—strêt, mn
strike—(hit)—gweskel, vb; (stop work) —scon-ober, mn; sconya-ober, vb
strong—crêf, adj
sugar—sucra, adj
suit—gwyscas, fn
supper—côn, mn
sweet—(of taste)—melys, adj; (of character)—whêk, adj
sweets—whegenow, mpln
swim—nuvya, vb

T

table—môs, fn
take—kemeres, vb; take off clothes—tenna dy'sky dyllajon
talk—cows, vb
tall—hŷr, adj
taste—blas, mn; I can taste fish—mŷ a glew blas pyskes; It tastes of fish—Ymâ blas pyskes warnodhe
tasty—blasus, adj
tea—(drink)—tê, mn; (meal)—côn, fn
teach—dysky, vb; I teach them Cornish—Mŷ a'wra dysky Kernewek dhedha
team—para, mn
thanks—murasta! excl.
they—ŷ, prn
thin—tanow(not fat), adj; (not thick)—môn, adj
think—predery, vb; crysy, vb
thirst—seghes, mn; I'm thirsty—Ymâ seghes dhym
throw—tewlel, vb
ticket—tokyn, mn; ticket office—tokynva, fn
tie—colm conna, mn; kelmy, vb
time—amser, mn; termyn, mn; 3 times—têrgwyth, adj; How many times?—Pescwyth? What time is it—P'ur ŷu; until next time—y'n wyth aral
tin—(metal)—stên, mn; (container)—cafas, mn
toast—cras, mn; piece of toast—crasen, fn; crasa, vb
tomato—keraval, mn
tomorrow—avorow, adv
tooth—dans, mn
tourist—havyas, mn
town—trêf, fn
trade union—syndycas
train—trên, vb
travel—vŷaja, vb
tree—gwedhen, fn
trowsers—lavvak-hŷr, mn
tune—tôn, mn
turn—trêlya, vb; turn around—trŷ, vb

U

ugly—hager, adj
uncle—ewnter, mn
understand—convedhes, vb
unfortunately—y'n gwetha prŷs, adv
upstairs—(motion)—dhe'n soler, adv; (position)—y'n soler, adv

V

valley—nans, mn
very—(before adj.)—pur²; (after adj & adv)—fert, adv
village—(parish)—plû, fn; (churchtown)—treveglôs, fn
vinegar—aysel, mn
voice—lêf, fn

W

wake up—dyfuna, vb

Wales—Kembrŷ, fn
walk—kerdhes, vb
wall—mur, mn; (between rooms)—
  Parwys, mn; (between fields—fôs,
  fn
want—mynnes, vb; I want...—Ymá
  whans dhym a², ...
warm—tôm, adj
wash—golghy, vb; have a wash—
  omwolghy, vb; wash up—golghy'n
  lystry, vb
water—dowr, mn
watch—golyas, vb
watch—(timepiece)—uryer, mn
wave—ton, fn
weak—gwan, adj
wear—(put on)—gwysca, vb; wear (a
  cap)—degy (cappa) vb
welsh—kembrek, adj; Welsh language
  —Kembrek, mn
Welshman—kembro, mn
Welshwoman—kembres, fn
wet—glŷp, adj; glybya, vb
what?—pandra? intern. prn; (in
  answer to call)—P'yùa?; I know
  what I like—Mŷ a wôr an pyth á
  blek dhym; What's the matter?—
  Pandra' wher?
when?—P'ur? intern adv
where?—ple⁵?
which one?—pynýl?
white—gwyn, adj
wide—ledan, adj
wife—gwrêk, fn
wind—gwyns, mn
window—fénester, fn
wine—gwŷn, mn
woman—benen, fn
wood—(trees)—côs, mn; (timber)—
  pren, mn
word—gér, mn
work—whêl, mn; gwŷtha, vb
workman—oberor, mn; (labouring
  man)—oberwas, mn
world—bŷs, mn
write—scryva, vb

Y

year—bledhen, fn; year of age—blôth;
  this year—hevleny, adv; last year—
  warleny,
yellow—melen, adj
yes—not generally expressed—(see
  grammar); (in agreement)—Yâ
you—tŷ,(sg. prn); whŷ (pl. prn)
young—yowynk, adj

Z

Zebra crossing—trusfa, fn

Kernewek ·· English

A

a², prep—of
a-dermyn, adv—in time, punctually
a-dhewedhes, adv—recently
a-dhyghow, adv—on the right
a-dre, adv—from home
a-drus, adv&prep—across
a-dryf, (+dhe² with prns) adv-prep—behind
a-eseth, adv&adj—seated
agan(coll a'n) prn—our
agas ,(coll a's) prn—your (pl)
aghup, adj—busy
amanyn, mn—butter
amary, mn, pl—ow—cupboard
amser, mn, pl—ow—(1)time(2)tense of vb
a'n see agan
androw, mn&adv—evening, late afternoon
anes, adj—difficult
ara, adj—slow (of movement)
a-rak, adv prep—in front (of)
arbennek, adj—special
arghans, mn—(1)silver, (2) money
a's see agas
asclajen, fn, col. asclas—fried chips
asclatty, mn, pl—ow—fish & chip shop
ascorn, mn, pl-eskern—bone
assa, adj—second
aswon, vb—recognize
aswonvos, vb—know (a person)
attes. adj—comfortable (1)Attes ôs?—Are you c.? (2)Attes yu'n gadar dhys—Is the chair c. (for you)
a-ûgh, prep—above
a-var, adv—early
aven, fn pl. avennow—picture
a-vern, adj—interesting, relevant
avon, fn, pl avenow—river
avorow, adv—tomorrow
a-ys, prep—below

B

baban, mn, pl—as—baby
bagha, vb—catch
bakken, nm—bacon
balgh, adj—proud
bara,· mn—bread
bara 'manyn,—bread & butter →
bargen-tyr, mn, pl—yow-tyr—farm
ben, f prn—an ŷl...hŷ ben—the one...the other
benen, fn, pl—benenes—woman
ber, adj—short
bera, vb—drop

beryk, adj—fat
bewa, vb—live; bewa worth kês—live on cheese
bewnans, mn, pl—ow—life
blas—, mn, pl—ow—taste –cafos blas war²—enjoy
blasus, adj—tasty
bledhen, fn, pl—bledhynnow—year
blejen, fn, pl—blejyow—flower
blejewa, vb→flower, bloom
blew, mn—hair (of body) coat of animal
blôth, fn—year of age, pymp blôth—six years old
bo, conj—or
boghosek, adj—poor
bôs, vb—be
bôs, mn, pl—ow—food
botasen, fn, pl—botasow—boot
braf, adj—fine, brave
bras, adj—big
brassa, adj—bigger; an-brassa—the biggest
brêgh, fn, d. dywvrêgh, pl—yow—arm
broder, mn, pl—breder—brother
bron, fn, d. dywvron—pl. bronnau—breast
brongolm, mn, pl—ow—bra
bryjyon, vb—boil
bryn, mn, pl—yow—hill
bryntyn, adj—excellent
bowjy, mn, pl—ow—cow's house
bûgh, fn, pl-bûghas—cow
bûsty, mn, pl—ow—cafe, restaurant
byghan, adj—small
bys, mn, pl—ou—world
bys, mn, pl.—besyas—finger
bysow, mn, pl—bysewow—finger ring
bysy, adj—important

C

cadar, fn, pl cadêryow—chair
cafas, mn, pl—cafasow—cup(container)
cafe, mn—coffee—cafe scon—instant c.
cafos, vb—find, get
cales, adj—hard
caltor, fn, pl—yow—kettle
cam, adj—bent, crooked
cân, fn, pl—cânow—song
cana, vb—sing
canor, mn, pl—yon—singer
cans, num—hundred
canstel, fn, pl—low—basket
cansfledhen, fn, pl—cansfledhynnow—century
cappa—cap
cara, vb—love
caradow, adj—lovable, loving
carjy, mn, pl- ow—garage
carn, mn, pl—ow—hill, height
car-tân, mn, pl, kerry-tân—car, automobile
casa, vb—hate

casadow, adj—hateful, unpleasant
castel, fn, pl—castylly—castle
cath, fn, pl—cathas—cat
chambour, mn, pl—ow—bedroom
chapel, mn, pl—yow—chapel
chy, mn, pl—ow—house
chyster, mn—cyder
claf, adj—ill
clavjy, mn, pl—ow—hospital
clavjor, mn, pl—yon—male nurse
clavyjores, fn, pl—ow—nurse
cler, adj—clear
cleth, adj—left
Cleth, mn—North
cleves, mn, pl—yow—disease
clewes, vb—(1)hear(2)feel
clôf, adj—lame
clôgh, fn, pl—clêgh—bell
clok, mn, pl—ys—clock
clor, adj—(1)cool, fresh(2)moderate
codha, vb—fall
côf, mn, pl—covyon—memory
collel, fn, pl—now—knife
colm conna, mn—neck tie
colon, fn, pl-kellylly—knife
comolen, fn, pl—comolow, col comol—cloud
côn, mn, pl—yow—tea, supper
conna, mn, pl—connahow—neck
conteth, mn, pl—contethow—county
convedhes, vb—understand
coref, mn—beer
côs, mn, pl—ow—wood, forest
cosel, adj—quiet
costen, fn, pl—now—target, dart board
côswŷk, fn, pl—côswygow—forest
cota, mn, pl—cotow—coat
cota-starch, mn—raincoat
côth, adj—old
cough, adj—scarlet
covath, fn, pl—ow—record, memorial
covatha, vb—put on record
cowl, mn, pl—yow—soup
cowlwul, vb—complete
cows, vb—speak, talk
craghor, mn, pl—yon—snob
crambla, vb—climb
cras, mn—toast
crasen, fn—piece of toast
crêf, adj—strong
cres, mn, pl—ow—middle
cresyk, mn. pl—cresygow—potato crisp, chip
cro, adj—fresh
crôghen, fn, pl—crêghyn—skin
crowst, mn, pl—ow—croust
crys, mn, pl-yow—shirt, blouse
cryspows, fn, pl—ow—jacket
crysy, vb—believe
cuf, adj—kind
cul, adj—narrow
cûsca, vb—sleep

D

da, adj—good
dalleth, mn, vb—start
dans, mn, pl—dyns—tooth
darbary, vb—prepare
darras, mn, pl—ow—door
dascafos, vb—get back, recover
dascor, vb—give back, return
davas, fn, pl—devêsyow, col devês—
sheep
dedhewy, vb—promise
dedhewys, mn, pl—dedhewadow—promise
degêa, vb—shut
degemeres, vb—receive
degês, adj—closed
degy, vb—carry
dêhen, mn—cream
dêhen-yey, mn—ice cream
demedhy, vb—betrothe
demma, mn, pl—demmow—halfpenny
dên, mn, pl—yon—man
deneren, fn, pl—now—penny
deres, mn, pl—you—stair
desevos, vb—expect
dewas, mn, pl—dewosow—liquor,
alcoholic beverage
dewassa, vb—drink, tipple, booze
dewedhes, adj—late
deweth, mn, pl—dewedhow—end
dewetha, adj—last
Dew genes—goodbye
dewheles, vb—return, go/come back
dewotty, mn, pl—ow—pub
dha, prn—your, (sg.)
dhe', prep—to, at
dhe'ves, adv—away (motion)
dôns, mn, pl—donsyow—dance
donsya, vb—dance
dôr, mn—earth
dôral, mn, pl—low—potato
dôs, vb—come
dosparth, mn, pl—ow—class, form (of
pupils)
dowr, mn, pl—ow—water
dreghevel, vb,—build, raise
dres, prep—across, over
drôk, adj—bad, naughty
druth, adj—expensive
dry, vb—bring
du, adj—black
dur, vb—Ny'm dur—I don't care—;
Ny'gan dur—We're not bothered
dybry, vb—eat
dydal, adj—free of charge
dyfun, adj—awake
dyfuna, vb—wake up
dyghow, adj—right (i.e. not left)
Dyghow, mn—South
dygoweth, adj—lonely
dyllas, mn, pl— ow—garment
dynar, mn—penny (after numerals)
dysquedhes, vb—show
dysky, vb—learn

E

ebren, fn—sky
edhen, mn, pl—ydhyn—bird
ef, emph eêf—he it
elyas, fn, pl—ow—second

---

enep, fn, pl—enebow—face
eneval, mn, pl—es—animal
enys, fn, pl—enesow—island
êok, mn, pl êogas—salmon
erbyn, prep—against, er ow fyn—
againt me; er y byn—against him
êrgh, mn—snow
ês, adj—easy
esedha, vb—sit down
eskynlur, mn, pl—yow—platform (in
station)
eskys, mn, pl—yow—shoe
eva, vb—drink
ewn, adj—correct, right, fair
ewnter, mn, pl—ewntras—uncle
eysel, mn—vinegar

F

fêr, mn, pl—yow—fair show; Fêr
an Tyr—The Royal Cornwall
fénester, fn, pl—fenestrow—window
ferellyth, mn, pl—ferellydhyon—chemist
(pharmacist)
ferelly, mn, pl—ow—chemist's shop
fest, adv—very
festyna, vb—hurry
fethan, vb—beat, defeat
fethans, mn, pl—ow—defeat
flôgh, mn, pl—flêghes, col. flogholeth—
child
'fors fatel vo—anyhow
forth, fn, pl—fordhow—road
fôs, fn, pl—ow—wall (between fields)
frût, mn, pl—ys—fruit
frya, vb—fry
fyllel, vb—fail, lack, miss

G

galar, mn—ow—pain
gallos, vb—be able to
galow, mn—pall
ganow, mn, pl—ganewow—mouth
gans—with; by
gar, mn, d. dywar, pl—garrow—leg
garow, adj—rough
gasa, vb—leave, allow
Gast!—general swear word (Stronger
version—Gast an ast!
gay, adj—pleasant
gell, adj—light brown, tawny
geiwel, vb—call
gêr, mn, pl—yow—word
glân, adj—clean
glaw—rain
glôs, fn, pl—ôw—ache
glow, mn—coal
godhvos, vb—know (a fact)
godryga, vb—stay, lodge
gôl, fn, pl—yow—holiday
golghy, vb—wash
golok, fn, pl—gologow—look
golow, mn, pl—es—light
gols, mn—hair
gôlya, vb—celebrate
golyas, vb—watch
gorfenna, vb—finish
gorher, mn, pl—yow—lid cover
gorm, adj—dark brown
gorra, vb—put
gorsaf, mn, pl—gorsavow—railway
station

---

gortheby, vb—answer
gorthyp, mn, pl—gorthebow—answer
gortos, vb—wait
gour, mn, pl—gwêr—husband
govyn, mn, pl—now—question
growedha, vb—lie down
gul, vb—do
gutrêl, mn, pl—gutrolow—piece of
furniture
gwak, adj—empty
gwan, adj—weak
gwaya, vb—move
gwaya-myr, mn, pl—yow—film
gwaytyans, mn, pl—ow—hope
gwedhen, fn, col—gwyth—tree
gwêl, mn, pl—yow—tilled field, pitch
gweles, vb—see
gwell, adj—better
gwella, adj—best
gwella, vb—get better, improve
gwellhé, vb—make better
gwels, mn—grass
gwely, mn—ow—bed
gwely-dêth, mn—sofa
gwer, adj—green
gweres, mn&vb—help
gwertha, vb—sell
gwerthjy, mn, pl—ow—shop
gwesty, mn, pl—ow—hotel
gwrêk, fn, pl—gwrageth—wife
gwruthyl, vb—make
gwryas, vb—sew
gwyn, adj—white, light coloured
gwyn, mn, pl—ow—wine
gwyns, mn, pl—ow—wind
gwynsak, adj—blowy, windy
gwyr, mn, pl—yow—right, privilege
gwysca, vb—put on, dress in
gwyscas, fn, pl—ow—suit
gwysk, fn, pl—gwysoow—costume, dress
gwytha, vb—keep, guard
gwytha, vb—work
gwytha', fn, pl—ow—factory
gyla, M prn—an yl...y gyla—the one..
the other
gyllys, adj—gone

H

hager, adj—ugly
ha(g), conj—and
haneth, adv—tonight
hanow, mn, pl—hynwyn—name
havyas, mn, pl—havysy—tourist, emmet
hedhyu, adv—today
hanaf, mn, pl—hanavow—cup
hanafas, mn, pl—ow—cupful; hanafas
('nafas) tê—cup of tea
hansel, mn—breakfast
hanter, mn, pl—ôw—half
harow!, excl—help!
hedhes, vb—reach, pass
hêl, mn, pl—helow—hall
hens, mn, pl—y—path
hepken, adv—only
hevel, adj—like, similar
hogen, fn, pl—hogas—pasty
hôgh, mn, pl—as, col—môgh—pig
holan, mn—salt
honen, prn—self
hot, mn, pl—tow—hat

55

hothlas, mn, pl-ow—soft drink, pop
Howldhrevel, mn—East
huny, prn—one
hȳ, f prn—she, it
hȳr, adj—long, tall

J

jȳn, mn, pl-nys—engine, machine
jyn nyja, mn—aeroplane

K

kê, mn, pl-ow—Cornish hedge
kedryn, mn, pl-yow—quarrel
kedrynya, vb—quarrel
kefnysor, mn, pl-yon—policeman, ab.
kefnytlȳ, mn, pl-yow—police station
kefvewy, mn, party
kegyn, fn, pl-ow—kitchen
kelgh, mn, pl-ow—circle
keily, vb—lose, miss
kelorn, mn, pl-ow—bucket
kelmy(worth), vb—bind (to)
kembrek, adj—Welsh
Kembrek, non—Welsh language
kembres, fn, pl-ow—Welshwoman
kembro, mn, pl-kembry—Welshman
Kembry, fn—Wales
kemeres, vb—take
kemyskȳ, vb—mix
kénethel, fn, pl-kénethlow—nation
kénethlek, adj—national
kens, adv—before, formerly; kens del²
dheth—before he came
ker, adj—dear
kêr, fn, pl-row—city
keral, mn, pl-low—tomato
kerdhes, vb—walk
kerensa, fn—affection, friendship, love
keresyk, f&mn—(term of endearment to
child), dear, love
kernewek, adj—Cornish
kernewek, mn, pl-yon—Cornishman
Kernow, fn—Cornwall
kernowes, fn, pl-ow—Cornishwoman
kês, mn—cheese
kether, adj—good-looking, pretty
kettrȳnjȳ, mn, pl-ow—bus station
kettrȳnva, fn, pl-ow—bus stop
kevalavor, mn, pl-yon—capitalist
kevothak, adj—rich
keyn, mn, pl-ow—back
kyfȳth, mn—jam
kȳ, mn, pl-cun—dog
kyfvewy, col—company, gang, party
kȳk, mn, pl-kygow—meat
kȳl, mn, pl-kylyow—back (of hand,
house, page, etc)
kyttrȳn, mn, pl-yow—bus

L

lagas, mn, d. deulagas, pl-lagasow—
eye
lam, mn, pl-mow—jump
las, mn, pl-ow—drink
lavrak ber, mn, pl-lavrogow-ber—
pair of sheets
lavrak-bȳghan, mn—pair of drawers

lavrak-hȳr, mn—pair of trousers
lē, adj—less
ledan, adj—wide
lêf, mn, pl-levow—voice
len-gwely, mn, pl-now-gwely—blanket
lemmel, vb—jump
lemmyn, adv—now
lenna, vb—read
lent, adj—slow-witted
lenwel, vb—fill
lesky, vb—burn
lêth, mn—milk
leverel, vb—say
lewgh, mn—mist
lewyas, vb—steer, drive
lô, pl-yow—spoon
lôgh, fn, pl-loghow—lake
lôr, fn—moon
lost, mn, pl-ow—tail
losten, fn, pl-now—skirt
lowarth, mn, pl-ow—garden
lowen, adj—glad, happy
luf, fn, d. dywluf, pl-yow—hand
lugarn, mn, pl-lugern—lamp, light
lun—full
lur, mn, pl-yow—floor
lȳ, mn, pl-ow—dinner, lunch
lȳes, adj (t.sg.)—many
lȳha, adj—least
lyther, mn, pl-ow—letter
lytheren, fn, pl-now—letter of alphabet
lytherjȳ, mn, pl-ow-post office
lytherva, fn, pl-ow—sub-post office in
shop
lytherwas, mn, pl-lytherwêsyon—
postman
lyver, mn, pl-lyfrow—book

M

'm, prn—me, my
maglen-dân, fn, pl-now-tân—grate
mam, fn, pl-mow—mother
mam-wyn, fn, pl-mow-gwyn—grandmother
man, adv—at all
manek, fn, pl-manegow—glove
map, mn, pl-mêbyon—son
marnas, ma's, conj—only, but
margh, mn, pl-mêrghas—horse
marghas, fn, pl-you—market
martesen, adv—perhaps
mâs, adj—good
mâsgyow mpln—sweets
maw, mn, pl-mêbyon—lad, boy
medhow, adj—drunk
mêl, mn—honey
melen, adj—yellow
melys, adj—sweet-tasting
mên, mn, pl-meyn—stone, mineral
meneth, mn, pl-menedhyow—mountains
mes, conj—but
modryp, mn, pl-modrebeth—aunt
môn, adj—thin
mona, mn—charge, cash
mor, mn, pl-ow—sea
moren, fn, pl-moronyon—lass, maid,
young woman
môs, vb—go
môs, fn, pl-ow—table
mowes, fn, pl-mowysy—girl
moy, adj—more
moyha, adj—most

mur, mn, pl-yow—wall
mur, adj—great
mur a²—a lot of
murasta! —thanks
mȳ, prn—I
myldȳr, mn, pl-yow—mile
mynnes, vb—(1) wish, will to (2)
auxiliary vb. for future (see grammar)
mynwharth, mn, pl-ow—smile
mynwherthyn, vb—smile
mynysen, fn, col-mynys—minute
mȳras(worth), vb—look (at)
mȳs, mn, pl-mysow—month
mȳrjȳ, mn, pl-ou—cinema
myttyn, mn, pl-yow—morning

N

nâ—no
'nafas, fn, -coll.see hanafas
nans, fn, pl-ow—valley
nasweth, fn, pl-naswedhow—(1)needle
(2)hand of clock
nebonen, prn—someone
negys, mn, pl-ow—message
neppyth, prn—something
netra, f prn—nothing
new, fn, pl-yow—sink, washbasin
n'ewer, coll. see nyhewer
newl, mn—fog
newodhow, mpln—news
nôs, fn, pl-ow—night
nôth, adj—naked
noweth, adj—new, fresh
nowys, vb—change
nuvya, vb—swim
nȳ², nyns(before vowels in mones&
bones)—not
nyhewer, adv—last night
nyvera, vb—count

O

oberor, mn, pl-yon—worker
oberwas, mn, pl-oberwêsyon—labouring man
olew, mn—edible oil
oll, adj—all
omdhydhana, vb—enjoy oneself
omglewes, vb—feel
omma—here
omrewleth, fn—home rule
omrȳ, vb—give in, surrender
omwaya, vb—move (oneself)
omwolghy, vb—have a wash
omwysca, vb—put on (clothes), don
ôn, fn, pl-ênas—lamb
onen, pln—one
ow⁴, vrb prt—placed before von. to
form present participle
own, mn, pl-ow—fear
owr, mn, pl-ys—hour in reckoning time
owraval, mn, pl-low—orange
oy, mn, pl-ow—egg
oyl, mn—oil
oy, mn, pl-ow—egg

P

pâl, fn, pl-yow—spade
pandra²?, prn—what?
para, mn pl-rys—team

parwys, mn, pl-y—wall (between rooms)
paper, mn—paper
park, mn, pl-parcow—field, park
parusy, vb—make ready, prepare
parys, adj—ready
pawgen, fn, pl-sock
pell, adj & adv—far, for a long time
pellglew, mn, pl-yow—radio
penans, mn, pl-ow—penalty
perna, vb, coll—see prena
pen, mn, pl-now—head
person, mn, pl-tus—person
perth, fn, pl-perthy—bush, quickset
  hedge
perthy, vb—bear, sustain; p. own a²-
  fear; p. côf a²—remember
pesquwyth?. adv—how many times?
plas, mn, pl-yow—plate
ple²?—where?
plekya, vb—please; Ny blêk dhym—I
  don't like it
plôs, adj—dirty
plu, fn, pl-pluyow—parish
pluvak, fn, pl-pluvogow—pillow,
  cushion
pobas, vb—bake
podyk, mn, pl-podygow—jug
pon, mn—dust
pons, mn, pl-ow—bridge
ponya, vb—run
pôs, adj—heavy
pôsa, vb—lean
pôsek, adj—important
post, mn—post
pôth, adj—hot
potya, vb—kick
potyas, fn, pl-ow—kick
pow, mn, pl-yow—country
powes, mn, pl&vb—rest
pows, fn, pl-ow—frock, dress
prâs, mn, pl-prasow—meadow
predery, vb—think
pregeth, mn, pl-pregowthow—sermon
pren, mn, pl-yer—stick -limber
prena, vb—buy
pryosa, vb—marry
prys, mn, pl-ow—price
pryson, mn, pl-ow—jail
puber, mn—pepper
·pul, mn, pl-yow—piller, post
pup, adj—every
pupprys, adv—always
p'ur?—when?
pur, adj—pure
pur², adv—very
puptra, f prn—everything
pyctur. mn—picture
pynta, mn, pl-ow—pint
pynyl?—which one?
pys-da, adj—pleased
pys-drôk, adj—cross, annoyed
pysk, mn, pl-es—fish
pyskessa, vb—fish
pystyga, vb—ache
pyth, prn—which, what

R

raglen, fn, pl-now—apron
raglyen, fn, pl-now—programme (of
  events, society)
rak, prep—for, in order to
remenant, mn—rest, remainder
rencas, fn, pl-ow—social class; r-ober
  —working class

rês, mn—necessity; Rês yû dhym—I
  must
resek, vb—run
rôl, fn, pl-yow—list
rôl-bûs, fn—menu
rosen, fn, pl-now—rose
ry, vb—give
ruth, adj—red
ryblan, fn, pl-now—pavement
ryp, prep—by the side of
ryth, adj—free

S

sans, adj—holy
sarfor, mn, p,-yon—detective, secret
  policeman
sawgh, mn, pl-yow—trunk
sawghya, vb—pack
saws, mn, pl-on—Englishman
sawsnek, adj—English
sawsnek, .mn—English language
sawsnes, fn, pl-ow—Englishwoman
scaf, adj—light (not heavy)
scol, fn, pl-yow—school
scolober, mn—homework
scon-ober, mn, pl-yow-ober—strike
scovarn, fn, pl-dywscovarn, pl-
  scovarnow—(1)ear(2)handle (of jug,
  cup)
scram, mn, pl-mow—screen (T.V.
scryva, vb—write
scryvel, fn, pl-low—fountain pen, biro
scudel, fn, pl-low—dish
seban, mn—soap
sedhy, vb—sink
segh, adj—dry
segha, vb—dry
seghes, mn—thirst
seny, vb—sound, ring
sergh, mn—love
serrys, adj—angry
sêthen, fn, pl-now—dart
sevel, vb—stand up, stop
seythen, fn, pl-now—week
skew, fn, pl-yow—shelter, screen
snell, adj—fast
snod, mn, pl-ow—tape, ribbon, film
  (for camera)
soler, mn—upper part of house-y'n
  seler—upstairs (position); dhe'n s.—
  upstairs (motion)
sols, mn, pl-ow—shilling
sonblas, mn, pl-ow—disc, record
sonscryva, vb—record (on tape, disc)
sosyalek, adj—socialist
sows, mn, pl-ow—sauce
sowyny, vb—succeed, prosper
spâs, mn, pl-spasyow—opportunity
spyrys, mn, pl-yon—spirit, pisky
spysor, mn, pl-yon—grocer
sôdhva, fn, pl-ow—office
stên, mn—tin
stevel, mn, pl-yow—room
strêt, mn, pl-ow—street
strollas, mn, pl-ow—political party
sugra, mn—sugar r
syndycas, mn, pl-yow—trade union

T

tanow, adj—slim, thin
tâs, mn, pl-tasow—father
tâs-wyn, mn—grandfather
tê—tea
têk—handsome, beautiful, pretty
tenewan, mn, d. deudenewan, pl
  tenewennow—flank, side
tenna, vb—pull, draw
termyn, mn, pl-yow, time, season, term
terry, vb—break
têsen, fn, pl-now—cake
tevy, vb—grow
tew, adj—thick, fat
tewas, mn—sand
tewl, adj—dark
tewlder, mn—darkness
tewlel, vb—throw
tokyn, mn, pl-ow—ticket
tokynva, fn, pl-ow—ticket office
tom, adj—warm
ton, adj—warm
tôn, fn, pl-tonyow—tune
tor, fn, pl-row—belly
torn, mn, pl-ow—shift, core of work
torthyk, fn, pl-ow—loaf
torthyk, fn, pl-torthygow—split
towlen, fn, pl-now—programme,
  broadcast
travyth, f prn—nothing
trawythyow, adv—sometimes
trê, adv—at home
tredan, mn—electricity
trêf, fn, pl-trevow—town
trêf, fn, pl-treven—home
trêghy, vb—cut
trêlya, vb—turn, convert
tremena, vb—pass by, go past
trên, mn, pl-trenow—train
trêth, mn, pl-ow—beach
treveglôs, fn, pl-ow—churchtown
trôn, mn, pl-ow—nose
trôs, fn, d. dywdrôs pl-treys—foot
trusfa, fn, pl-ow—zebra crossing
tryga, vb—live, dwell
trygva, fn, pl-ow—address
trygys, adj—living
tryst, adj—sad
tu, mn, pl-yow—side, direction
tus, mpln—people, ow thus—my parents
tyller, mn, pl-yow—place (town,'village)
tylly, vb—pay
tyr²—three
tyr, mn, pl-yow—land
tyryen, fn, pl-yow—map

U

ûghel, adj—high, loud
un, num—one
unsel, adj—only
unverhe, vb—agree
unwyth—once
unyk, adj—lonely
ur, fn, pl-yow—hour of the clock, time
uryer, mn, pl-uryorow—watch
uthek, adj—awful, horrible

vodya, vb—depart
vỹach, mn, pl-vỹajow—journey
vỹaja, vb—travel

war²—on
warlérgh, prep—after; war⁺ow lergh-
   after me
whans, mn, pl-ow—desire
wharth, mn, pl-ow—laugh
wharthus, adj—funny
whegen, fn, sweet, pl—now (form of address), love,
   darling
whegyn, mn—sweet (form of address), love,
   darling
whejalen, fn, pl-whejalow—boil
whêk, adj—gentle, sweet
whêl, mn,pl-yow—work, works
wherthyn, vb—laugh
whethel, mn, pl-whethlow—story
whoer, fn, pl-wheryth—sister
whỹ, prn—you(pl)
worteweth, adv—at last, in the end
wosa, prep—after

ŷ, prn—they
ya—yes
yagh, adj—healthy
yar, fn, pl-yêr—hen
yeghes, mn—health
yet, fn, pl-tow—gate
yêth, fn, pl-ow—language
yeuny (warlérgh), vb—long (for) look
   forward (to)
yey, mn—ice
yeyn, adj—cold
yeynder, mn—cold
ygery, vb—open
ygor, adj—open
ŷl, prn—an ŷl...ŷ gŷla—the one...the
   other
ylyn, adj—clear, pure
yn, prep—in, at
yndella, adv—thus, in that way
yndelma, adv—thus, in this way
yn le vyth, adj—anywhere
yntra, prep (before vowels yntei)—
   between
yn-trê, adv—at home, in
yn-tro, adv—back
ynwêth, adv—so, as well
yonk, adj coll. see yowynk
yowynk, adj—young
ythô, conj—then, now, well

DEDHYOW–Days

Dê Sul–Sunday
Dê Lun–Monday
Dê Merth–Tuesday
Dê Mergher–Wednesday
Dê Yow–Thursday
Dê Gwener–Friday
Dê Sadorn–Saturday

MÝSOW–Months

Mŷs Genver–January
Mŷs Whevrer–February
Mŷs Merth–March
Mŷs Ebrel–April
Mŷs Mê–May
Mŷs Metheven–June
Mŷs Gortheren–July
Mŷs Est–August
Mŷs Gwyngala–September
Mŷs Hedra–October
Mŷs Du–November
Mŷs Kevardhu–December

TERMYNOW–Seasons

Gwaynten–Spring
Hâf–Summer
Kynyaf–Autumn
Gwâf–Winter

TYLLERYOW, TYROW, AVENOW
–Places, Countries, Rivers

Alban, fn–Scotland
Almayn, fn–Germany
An Grŷben, fn–Cribben Point
An Tyreth Ûghel –North Cornwall
Bodmenêgh, fn–Bodmin
Brôn Wennyly–Brown Willy
Breten, fn–Britain

Breten Vŷghan, fn–Brittany
Cambrôn, fn–Camborne
Caradon, fn–Caradon
Carrek, fn–Carrick
Carrek Lôs y'n Côs–S. Michael's
 Mount
Carn Golowva, mn–Carn Galver
Densher, fn–Devon
Deveren, fn–Devoran
Dewnans, fn–Dumnonia (ancient Celtic
 kingdom from Land's End to Somerset
 & Dorset)
Dunheved, mn–Lanson/Lanceston
Fawy, fn–Fowey
Gwlâs an Hâf, fn–Somerset
Henlŷs, mn–Helston
Hayl, mn–Hayle
Havren, fn–Severn
Kêr Esk, fn–Exeter
Kerrŷer, fn–Kerrien
Kŷl Margh, mn–Kilmar
Kembry, fn–Wales
Kernow, fn–Cornwall
Landrêth, fn–S. Blazey
Lansant, fn–Lezant
Lanûst, fn–S. Just & Laneast
Lodenek, fn–Padsta/Padstow
Lôgh, fn–Looe
Lok Sulyen, mn–Luxulyan
Lulyn, fn–Newlyn
Lŷs Kerya, mn–Liskeard
Manow, fn–Isle of Mann
Menêghek, fn–Meneague
Mor Breten, mn–The Channel
Moresk, fn–Fal- Truro river complex
Pen an Wlâs, mn–Land's End
Pen Sans, mn–Land's End
Penwyth, mn–Penwith
Pons Mur, mn–Grampound
Pons Noweth, mn–Ponsanooth
Porth, mn–Par
Porth Ya, mn–S. Ives
Pow Frŷnk, mn–France
Pow Saws, mn–England
Sêghla, mn–Zelah
Syllan, fn–Scilly
Towan Porth Lystry, mn–New Quay
Ysalmayn, fn–Netherlands
Ywerdhon, fn–Ireland

59

Also from Y Lolfa . . .

THE PAN-CELTIC PHRASEBOOK
William Knox
Unique phrasebook for the main four Celtic languages, with French and English.
0 86243 441 6
£5.95

THE CELTIC VISION
John Meirion Morris
Handsome, large-format book presenting a new, spiritual interpretation of Celtic art.
0 86243 635 4
£19.95

CELTIC DAWN
Peter Berresford Ellis
A lively and amusing
history of the Pan-Celtic
movement.
0 86243 643 5
£9.95

THE CELTIC REVOLUTION
Peter Berresford Ellis
An essential Pan-Celtic
primer describing the six
Celtic nations' fight for
survival.
0 86243 096 8
£7.95

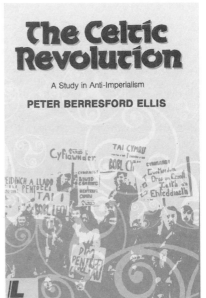

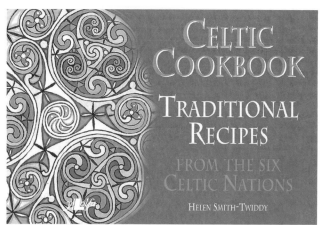

CELTIC COOKBOOK
Helen Smith-Twiddy
Traditional recipes
from the six Celtic
nations.
0 86243 641 9
£4.94

ETERNAL WALES
Marian Delyth and Gwynfor Evans
A beautiful, coffee-table book with
stiking images and text invoking Welsh
history.
0 86243 608 7
£24.95

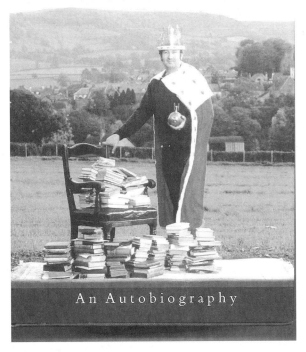

MY KINGDOM OF BOOKS
Richard Booth
The candid, anarchic autobiography of
the King of second-hand bookselling.
0 86243 495 5
£14.95

For a full list of our Celtic and
general publications, ask for your
free copy of our new Catalogue –
or simply surf into our secure
website, **www.ylolfa.com**,
where you may order on-line.

TALYBONT, CEREDIGION, CYMRU (WALES) SY24 5AP
ebost ylolfa@ylolfa.com
gwefan www.ylolfa.com
ffôn (01970) 832 304
ffacs 832 782